Houseplants Are Houseguests

Tips for Indoor Garden Success

Brain cactus

Anne Moore

Illustrated by Rebecca Saunders

Houseplants Are Houseguests: Tips for Indoor Garden Success

Published by Wheatmark®
610 East Delano Street, Suite 104, Tucson, Arizona 85705 U.S.A.
www.wheatmark.com

ISBN: 978-1-60494-464-8
LCCN: 2010930442

Contents

Contents

3. In the Comfort Zone

4. Odd Fellows

5. The Shopper in You

Introduction

Gloxinia

A collection of houseplants is a gathering of personalities, as different from each other as people can be. In our homes, they are our guests.

Some are friendly, rewarding, and fun to have around. Others are troublesome and frustrating to live with. Some thrive; others just survive. The best way to care for a plant is to understand its origins on Earth and to try to duplicate nature in providing what it needs. The mantra "Think of your plants as people" reigns over all. You won't go wrong.

The essays in this collection are adapted from my newspaper column and magazine articles in which I have tried to share my own experience as an amateur grower in the Northeast, although houseplants can and do flourish in every climate zone. If this approach has helped my readers tackle plant care with confidence and a sense of humor and avoid some of the mistakes I have made (and I have made plenty), so much the better! I am neither a botanist nor a Master Gardener. I am just someone who loves plants and loves to write about them.

These selected articles have been organized as a sort of pathway leading the reader from the basics of plant care, through the joys of a job well done, and to a higher challenge in trying something new and different.

The line drawings have been done for this book by my friend Rebecca Saunders, an artist and photographer who also loves plants.

Thanks to Mary Moore for her good advice and technical assistance. And special thanks to my husband, Don, who built me a greenhouse, plumbed a propagation bench, wired grow lights, hauled around heavy pots, and happily accepted plants as permanent houseguests!

1

About the Basics

Houseplants Are Houseguests

A houseplant guide is full of useful tips. But I have found that all of the tips I use fall under one large umbrella that I call my eleventh commandment: "Think of your plants as people." Thinking of my plants as people helps me sense what they want, rejoice when they show signs of being content, and grieve when I cannot provide what they seem to need.

Plants are living creatures, like us. They are born, breathe, have a life span, and die. While on this earth, they live in the same atmosphere as we do; they are hot or cold, dry or wet, tough or tender. In the wild, plants have adapted to their habitats over the centuries, enabling them to survive in conditions that would kill many of us humans.

From the arctic tundra to the tropical rainforests, plants take what they need from their natural surroundings. The hot, desert plants have evolved to be water storage tanks, holding moisture in their thick stems to be absorbed as needed. On the other hand, the thin, huge leaves of tropical forest plants give up moisture over a broad expanse to keep the plant cool. The wide variety of plant life all over the planet is witness to the principle that plants, left to their own devices in their own habitats, will do just fine.

The problem comes when they are taken out of their habitats and brought into ours. With their controlling devices no longer needed, they are at our mercy. This is when we must think of our houseplants as houseguests, especially as guests that we really want to have around for longer than three days!

Our houseguests need water, but they don't want to be drowned. They need light, but they don't want to be burned. They need good air circulation, but they don't want to be in a wind tunnel. In hot-climate conditions, being considerate is even more important, whether the houseguests are inside or out. If I am hot, so are they. They might want a little more to drink. A cool shower under the garden hose would feel good and be good for them, allowing more water to enter their systems through the leaves. If I would like a cool breeze during the day, so would they. A place under the shade of a tree or hanging from a low bough would allow more air to flow around them. They get hungry less frequently than I do, but they need regular feedings and extra nourishment during a period of fast growth. In colder climates and indoors for the winter, they need to be snuggled together to provide humidity and share enough light to stay happy.

If I am bothered by bugs, so are they. Although their bugs are different from my bugs, theirs can be even more dangerous, eventually eating away the leaves or sucking their juices. I must watch carefully for pests and react accordingly. Dousing them frequently under the hose or the spray from the kitchen sink will help wash away tiny eggs and keep the leaves fresh, but I may have to spray with an insecticide to eliminate an infestation—after spraying myself to ward off the mosquitoes!

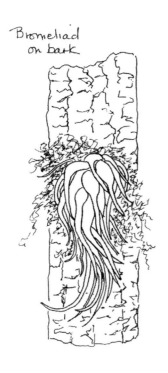

Bromeliad on bark

If I don't like crowds, neither do they. They need room to relax, to allow their stems and leaves to move freely, and to allow air movement for breathing. And now we come to what has been a standing joke for years—you should talk to your plants! Is this really a joke? We exhale carbon dioxide. Plants inhale carbon dioxide as part of the process of photosynthesis. If I stand over a plant and talk to it for a long time, I am providing it with some extra carbon dioxide. In small doses it may make no difference, but when I have a garden club meeting in my living room ... !

Just as immigrants have settled in America, plants have arrived in the New World and Europe from far-off lands. Gathered by the plant hunters and explorers and collected by the wealthy landowners of the last century, many of our houseplants still find themselves to be strangers in terms of their living conditions. To care for them well, it is important, once again, to think of them as people and to provide living conditions as close as possible to those they came from. Therefore, our houseguests from tropical rainforests will appreciate warmth, lower light levels, and humidity, whereas those from arid desert environments will respond to infrequent waterings and strong light.

It is also helpful to know about the origins of plants so that we may come as close as possible to duplicating their original living conditions. This becomes crucial in the so-called short day plants, like the poinsettia and the Christmas cactus, which require longer periods of darkness in order to set their buds. This is only one example of how a plant's origin has an influence over its behavior and why it is important to know its history.

There is only one scenario that I have experienced in which this eleventh commandment doesn't quite work, and that is when I want to get rid of a plant. If it is sickly or diseased, no problem—I'll put it out of its misery. But if it is healthy, vibrant, and in its prime, I'll have to come up with some excuse. There's no reason why a houseguest can't be moved along to visit someone else.

Does anyone want an extra jade plant?

Let's Talk About Pots

Early on, I became convinced that there were only two permissible kinds of pots to hold good-looking plants: terra cotta and green plastic—nothing else would do. Until just recently, I have clung to that mind-set, being of the conviction that a beautiful plant should be the decoration, not the pot. In other words, if you have worked hard to grow a perfect specimen, why should you provide a distraction and allow anyone to pay attention to anything else? Beyond the distraction factor are the strong negative impressions from unattractive pots. All you have to do to destroy the beauty of a hanging plant is to put it into white plastic!

Recently, I have come to appreciate another look, and with it comes a change in attitude. It's connected to the boom in garden accessories over the last few years, and especially to the proliferation of ceramics in pots and decorative elements for the garden. Recent articles on containers proclaim that the pot is half of the presentation, and I must admit that this is truer today than it ever used to be.

While traveling in Italy, I was enchanted with local ceramics and especially the anthropomorphic vases of the Sicilians. Faces meant to be those of gods and goddesses smiled dreamily, glowered darkly, or simply stared into space. Painted with the bright colors of the Mediterranean, they were wonderful examples of a traditional art form and, I thought, would be super to have in one's home and used as cachepots. Only gradually did I accept the notion that a plant growing out of the top of a god's head could be rather

7

cute! Imagine Athena with hair of curly parsley or Odysseus with a crew cut of thick, green grass!

The ceramics of our own Southwest are equally delightful, using strong primary colors and featuring the traditional designs of Latin American cultures. Large vases, slim chimneys, and whimsical pots abound in garden centers. Terra cotta burros, coyotes, rabbits, and javelinas are everywhere, usually planted with cacti and succulents. Beautiful, large terra cotta pots are embellished with designs of swags, fruits and vegetables, and ribbons. Many have patterns cut and etched into the clay. Usually produced in Mexico, they come in a wide variety of sizes and shapes, and most are quite inexpensive.

Shopping around for summer containers is an eye-opening adventure. The garden accessory business must be booming as new designs appear in garden shops and are featured in catalogs. But before springing for whatever appeals to the eye, remember that whatever goes into the pot must be cared for, and the properties of the pot itself have a lot to do with that care.

One word of caution about all types of pots. There must be a way to provide drainage for the planting medium. Be sure that there is at least one hole in the bottom of the pot. Drill one if there isn't. If you want to insert a pot into a decorative container, place a layer of pebbles between the two, and monitor your watering so that the pot containing the plant does not end up sitting in water.

Here follows a brief rundown of the principal types of pots and how they will perform for you.

Terra Cotta

The name comes from the Italian "baked earth," and that is what it is. Clay vessels are fired to a high temperature, which is one of the determinants of the quality of the pot. Although many are quite inexpensive, better quality pots fired to higher temperatures cost more but tend to last longer. Offerings in catalogs can range from under one hundred dollars to over one thousand dollars!

All terra cotta pots are porous, losing moisture through their sides, which means that you must water their plants more frequently. They also tend to draw salts and minerals outward to their surface, which can cause stains, although there are ways of treating this. They are more fragile, can crack, and must be brought inside for the winter in cold climate zones, but they are beautiful!

CERAMIC

These are glazed clay pots that can hold moisture longer than their unglazed cousins. Cobalt blue is a popular and dramatic color, showing up not only in glazed pots, but also in birdbaths and a variety of spheres, cubes, and other garden ornaments. Pale green and brown glazes may be easier to work with, however, when choosing plants for a container. The possibilities for decorative treatment are endless.

FIBERGLASS AND PLASTIC

This probably is the most practical material with many advantages. Plastic pots can be moved and carried easily. They do not lose moisture and can be left outdoors during the winter. The darker colors can fade in sunlight, however, and plastic can bend or crack with wear. Fiberglass is insulating, maintaining a more constant temperature in the planting medium.

Imitation terra cotta in a lightweight fiberglass has been on the market for quite a while, but manufacturers seem to be getting better at the imitation. It truly is hard to tell the difference until you get up close. Colors range from the traditional red to white and tan, imitating the various shades of terra cotta, and decorative motifs closely resemble the real thing. And fiberglass pots are much less expensive than terra cotta.

WOOD

This is a good choice for certain kinds of plants, especially small trees and shrubs, or to give a rustic appearance. Unless treated with a waterproof sealer, wood is porous and will require more frequent watering. It is durable and will not chip or crack. Allowing air to circulate underneath the container will help it last longer and provide drainage.

STONE OR CONCRETE

Obviously durable. These are heavy to carry and not easily moved once planted. Many give an Italianate look to a formal garden, or they can be quite whimsical depending on the design. They can be expensive but will last. I have a small concrete "twelve apostles pot," looking like a mini medieval baptismal font, which was purchased at least twenty years ago and which I replant every summer. It will outlive me!

Hold the Water

There is no action that is more important to the proper care of house-plants than watering. And there is no action that causes more harm when done the wrong way. And there is no action that is more commonly done the wrong way.

It certainly is true that every living creature needs water, but needs vary. The quickest way to ruin your plants is to kill 'em with kindness in the form of overwatering.

Every houseplant guide describes the amount of water needed by the different species. Some plants want their soil to be kept constantly moist, while others want to dry out between waterings. A clue to these differ-ent needs lies in the plants' origins. Many of our common houseplants originated in the tropics where they had plenty of moisture either from rainfall or the humidity in the air. Others originated in deserts where they received copious amounts of water only during the rainy season. These clues tell us how much and how.

As always, the best way to think about watering is to think of our plants as people. A 250-pound football player is going to need a lot more water than a 100-pound granny in a rocking chair. But there is an op-posite effect in the world of plants. A large root ball will hold moisture longer than a very small one. And a plant's size, location in the house, rate of growth, and age can determine how much water it requires.

Each plant is an individual. Tall or short, big or little, thick or thin, in the sun or in shade, in clay pots or in plastic—each plant has its individual needs for a certain amount of water or, better said, moisture. One size does not fit all—anymore than one bottle of water provides the same needs for a tennis player in ninety-degree heat as it does for someone lying in a hammock in the shade.

When I fill up my watering can, I think of that old song about Hard-Hearted Hannah "pouring water on a drowning man!" Think of that drowning man when you test your plant's soil, and more often than not you will leave it alone. We get clues by looking at the soil in the pot and feeling it. If the top of the surface looks a little crusty and begins to develop small cracks, it's getting dry. But hold off! Houseplant roots generally lie in the bottom two-thirds of the pot. Forget that new manicure and stick your finger into the pot to see if you feel any moist soil. If you do, wait another day and test again before watering. (This finger test also helps you determine whether your root ball is becoming too compacted. If it is, you may need to repot the plant.)

Water meters are readily available in garden centers and will give you a "dry, moist, or wet" readout. But they have a shelf or use life, and can become unreliable if the tips are damaged by scratching or scraping.

The other extreme is allowing the soil to dry out too much. If it starts to pull away from the sides of the pot, it is getting very dry. The plant will tell you that it's thirsty with wilting foliage and brown leaf edges and tips. If the condition becomes this drastic, the root ball may need a good soaking. Instead of watering from the top, plunge the pot into a tub and keep it there until bubbling ceases. Then drain it thoroughly, being careful not to let the pot sit in leftover water.

It's not just the amount of water; it's the technique of watering that makes the difference between thriving and barely surviving. Some people use bottom watering to ensure that the entire soil mass will get its share. Place the pot in a pan of water and wait until the surface of the soil becomes moist. Then drain it well. If any salts accumulate on the surface, scrape them off lightly and dust with fresh planting medium.

Talking technique brings us to methods of watering and another chance to think of our plants as people. You would not like to get wet on just one side. It's important to disperse the water into the entire root ball,

not just one side of it. Turn the pot to get the water evenly spread. Try not to get the foliage wet—this is a leading cause of fungus, just like toes kept too long in wet boots. Water in the morning so that the foliage will be thoroughly dry by evening, when pests might be more tempted to invade. You would not like to sit in the bathtub all day, so don't let your pot sit in water either. This is a leading cause of root rot. Providing good drainage is an essential aspect of good watering.

Now what about the water itself? Some municipal water supplies contain fluoride and chlorine, which may cause leaf tip browning in certain plants. If this seems to be a problem, fill up a large container with tap water and let it sit overnight to evaporate and eliminate these minor chemicals. If your home has a water softener system, try to collect rain water and melted snow to use as often as possible.

Where homes are heated during the winter, humidifiers provide valuable moisture for the health of both people and plants. If you use a dehumidifier you will receive a valuable side benefit in that it produces distilled water that the plants will love.

And if you go away for a winter vacation? I've not yet found an automatic watering system that works to my satisfaction. I'll try again but, in the meantime, I have someone who will come in and NOT water my plants!

Philodendron— Best for Beginners

M y first plant probably was a philodendron, although I cannot remember it. Probably it was in my college room, struggling to stay alive in darkness and drought. That's what they do, these philodendrons— stay alive, the characteristic that makes them everyone's favorite beginner plant.

It's too bad that philodendrons have this reputation, because it induces an expectation that they are impossible to kill (false), and that they will pull through, no matter what (also false). The fact is that a philodendron is a truly wonderful beginner's plant because it demonstrates the noticeable difference between a well-grown plant and one that is just getting by. The strugglers are the ones we see hanging over our heads in the dry cleaner's or plunked in the dimmest corner of the doctor's waiting room. The beginner can see that long straggling stems and dusty leaves are not attractive and, as a result, will be inspired to grow a healthy philodendron the right way!

The simple heartleaf philodendron, *P. scandens*, provides a good example of how to approach basic houseplant care, which is to duplicate the plant's native conditions as closely as possible. Philodendrons are tropical rainforest plants, growing either on the forest floor or twining their way up a tree toward the light but still staying under the canopy. They prefer filtered bright light or a steady medium light. They obviously love humidity, but today's cultivars have evolved to tolerate fairly dry indoor air. They like household temperatures above seventy degrees, with a ten-degree drop at night. They like to dry out a little between waterings and enjoy a regular diet of feedings during their growing periods.

So why isn't this the easiest regimen in the world? It is. The good and bad news is that the philodendron will let you know how unhappy it is in obvious ways when conditions become too tough. It will become a stemmy, straggly specimen with scrawny leaves if it does not get enough light. Its leaves will turn yellow if overwatered, and they will brown and fall off if underwatered. It likes to have its leaves kept clean and free of dust so that it can breathe easily and keep that chlorophyll coming. In this sense, it is a good patient for the beginner caretaker. It will make its needs known before it becomes too late to correct the problems.

The botanical name *Philodendron* evolved from Greek and means "lover of trees," thereby describing the vining type that races up tree trunks in the jungles of Central and South America and some Caribbean islands. This type is one of the world's most commonly grown houseplants, but it should be recognized that a vine wants to climb up or around or on something. Left on its own in a pot, and especially a hanging pot, the vining stem will reach out for something to grab hold of. If it doesn't find anything, it will just hang in midair, becoming stemmy and spindly as it hunts for support. A few little trailers are fine and can be charming against a window or filling up a corner, but that's enough. It's therefore best to keep it pruned back in its pot so that bushier growth will occur. The plant's form will then be visually pleasing, and it will be healthy.

Another approach is to give the vine something to climb on. A hoop or a trellis or a piece of wood set into the pot as a backdrop will work. Given good growing conditions, this vine should really take off. We can control the speed and route, encouraging the vine to grow in any desirable pattern—up and around a window, across a beamed ceiling, mixing it up with books on a bookshelf. Even here, however, it should be kept pruned back and under control.

As the stem grows, tiny aerial roots are often produced. They can be trained to cling to the support device or just be tucked back into the soil of the pot where they will take hold and produce new plantlets. We can help them to do this by wounding, or cutting into, the stems slightly where they touch the surface, and then fastening them down with hairpins or paper clips opened up to make little hoops. Keep the soil surface moist. That wounded spot should produce roots and, eventually, new little plants, turning your original plant into a shrub or giving you the opportunity to increase your collection.

Other philodendron types grow in clusters of leaves coming up from the crown of the plant. They are called self-heading philodendrons, and they are also good houseplants, requiring the same care as the *P. scandens*. The saddle-leafed philodendron, *P. selloum*, has deeply lobed leaves, and the variety 'Burgundy' is named for its reddish stems and foliage. Both grow to a large size; the saddle-leafed can get to be three to four feet tall.

Another large plant commonly called a split-leaf philodendron or Swiss Cheese plant because of the holes in its leaves is not a philodendron at all, but belongs to a different species. This is *Monstera deliciosa*. Don't let its Latin name scare you away! If you have enough space for it, you'll love it.

Have Fun with Seeds

Starting seeds indoors for your vegetable garden or for your summer containers is smart, fun, and thrifty. Start in time to allow the two to three weeks that most seeds require for germination and the four to six weeks needed to grow them before moving them outdoors. It all sounds so simple until you walk into your local garden supply store and come face-to-face with everything you were afraid to know about seeds!

So many germination aids! So many choices in equipment, kits, and mediums. To peat pot or not! And do I really need heating cables and grow lights?

The answer is to look at how Nature does it, and imitate it as best you can. I have found that the "window greenhouse" design works well. It's a rectangular tray that holds several six-pot starter flats and comes with a plastic cover to keep in the moisture. Or just use a few of your plastic pots and cover with baggies, propped up by the plant labels or small wooden skewers to prevent the plastic from touching the emerging seedlings. All you really need is soil, light, and water, and the seeds' natural drive to sprout will do the rest. Everything else is secondary, but may be helpful depending on conditions in your home.

To begin, check the seed packets to see if soaking or scarifying (scratching the surface) is required prior to setting them, and follow the directions. Use a soilless mix, and pop one to three seeds, depending on their size, in each little starter pot. You will have a much higher success rate if you

sprinkle a thin layer of milled sphagnum moss over the seeds. It provides aeration to the soil surface and is sterile, thereby helping to prevent damping-off disease, which can destroy the tiny stems of emerging seedlings. Sow the minuscule seeds of petunia and alyssum directly into the moss. It is available at garden supply stores, is inexpensive, and a little goes a long way.

Set the flats or pots in a pan of lukewarm water to draw moisture up through the planting medium without disturbing the tiny seeds. Use a mister to spray the surface with a fine mist of lukewarm water. If you use larger pots, place a thin layer of pebbles or broken crockery in the bottom before filling with soil to provide some drainage. Drain the flats after moistening, and set them in a place where they will receive bright light, but not direct sun, at least to begin with.

Label each flat with the name of the plant and the date the seeds were sown. You may think you will recognize the young seedlings for what they are, but a lot of them look amazingly alike, and later on you will want to identify them.

The best guide to starting seeds is to imitate nature as much as possible. The ground is warming up; therefore, the seeds do well with some bottom heat supplied with a heating cable, if you have one, or by placing the flat on top of the refrigerator or some other warm surface. Spring rains are gentle (or should be!). Use a mister or fine spray to water, or continue to bottom water. The sun is not too strong as yet—low to moderate light is desirable at first, especially while the flat is covered with plastic. Otherwise, the seeds could cook before they sprout.

Once seedlings emerge, remove their plastic coverings and give them direct sunlight. When the second set of leaves is established, transplant the seedling into an individual pot using the soil mix appropriate for its species. These are babies—handle with care! Hold each one gently by a leaf—not the stem, which is easily damaged. Work the tiny root system free with a pencil or skewer tip and have a small hole ready in the new pot to drop the seedling into. If space is limited, give preference to those that appear strongest with firm stems and good roots. Begin a feeding and

20

watering schedule appropriate for the species, and gradually move them into bright light or full sunlight, again depending on the species.

Move them into the garden or outdoor containers when the last danger of frost has passed. It helps to let them spend a few days in a cold frame or in a chilly part of your basement or garage to get acclimatized before setting them out. Just like people, they don't want a sudden shock to the system.

Christmas Cactus for All Seasons

Q: When is a cactus not a cactus?

A: When it's a Christmas cactus.

Right. It's not a cactus. But that doesn't matter, does it? Unless you're a taxonomist, and most of us aren't. Technically not a member of the huge cactus family, this plant nevertheless has had trouble finding any other name to go by. It looks like a cactus, so that's that!

Schlumbergera bridgesii and *S. truncata* are the Christmas and Thanksgiving cacti respectively. And to confuse things further, a late spring bloomer is totally different, a *Rhipsalidopsis gaertneri*, or Easter cactus!

Trying to identify these plants by their correct names is like climbing onto a merry-go-round of nomenclature, crossbreeding, and learning about the timetables used to force these plants into bloom for the commercial market. The latter may be the problem. Not to be picky, but I refuse to go along with the general "holiday cactus" label that attempts to cover them all. There are differences in these plants, even as there still are different holidays celebrated by every religion and nation, so *vive la difference*!

Fading in my pot right now is *S. truncata*, which was glorious with bright coral flowers and a low, spreading form. Called the crab cactus once upon a time, this plant has jointed stems with small hooks that look like the spines on a true cactus. By contrast, *S. bridgesii* is smooth and spineless and can grow quite large with arching, drooping stems. Both *S. truncata* and *S. bridgesii* have flattened joints and glossy surfaces, which make them interesting foliage plants when not in bloom. But the blooming period for them is a wow! The flowers are many-petalled and tubular in shape, and they come in bright colors of pink, cerise, coral, white, and rose. The Easter cactus produces pink to red flowers later in springtime.

These plants do well in average indoor temperatures with bright light or some periods of direct sunlight. Keep the soil evenly moist and feed with a balanced fertilizer (20-20-20) once a month. They enjoy summer outdoors in dappled sunlight or light shade. September is the month when they require special attention. In order to produce buds for the next season, they must have a long period of darkness every night for at least six weeks and/or a cold period.

Schlumbergera is one of a group of short-day plants that insist on re-minding themselves, and us, that they really belong in the tropics where the longer hours of darkness in early fall have a lot to do with their bloom-ing cycle. The pickiest of these short-day plants is the poinsettia, which demands total darkness in order to set its buds. Even a small break in this routine will result in green bracts, rendering it worthless as a Christmas gift! Unlike the poinsettia, however, *Schlumbergera* will produce buds re-

Christmas Cactus

gardless of the light cycle if the night-time temperature falls into the fifties. The best way to respond to these special needs is to leave the plant outdoors in the fall right up until the first frost. Stop feeding it, and water it very sparingly. It should have a generous set of buds when you bring it indoors where you can re-sume your regular schedule of watering and feeding. If properly cared for, *Schlumbergera* can live to a ripe old age.

It is easy to propagate these plants. Cut off a section of the stem just below one of the joints, leaving at least three sections on the cutting in a sort of Y shape. That joint is a node of the plant from which new growth occurs and contains the cells that will form roots. Moisten the tip of the joint with water, and dip it in a hormone rooting powder such as Roo-tone, available at garden centers. (Remember that these powders have a shelf life, so a fresh supply will produce the best results.) Shake off the excess powder, and set the cutting in moist builders sand (not beach sand) or whatever medium you like to use. Keep the cutting moist with misting, or cover the entire pot with plastic to make your own little greenhouse. When the joint sends out a set of strong little roots, pot up the cutting in your favorite houseplant soil mix.

This cutting is a clone that will be another Thanksgiving cactus or Christmas cactus or Easter cactus—just like its parent. You may be the only one who knows the difference or cares! Why not start a collection of all three for a nonstop six-month holiday season?

2

Getting Inspired

Veltheimia

Cyclamen—Touching Elegance

I will never get over my awe of the cyclamen. What is it about this plant that is so gorgeous that it seems unreal, almost artificial? The flowers are dramatic in their shape, with petals that bend and curve upward supported on strong slender stems. The colors are intense. The foliage is a show in itself; the heart-shaped leaves are a dark green with light veining and a spiderweb-patterned border along the edge with lighter green highlights toward the center. Put all these attributes together, and you have a winner with appeal for everyone.

Cyclamen persicum has been around for a long time, going back centuries in Europe where it was used as a medicinal plant for a variety of ailments, including baldness! As cyclamens have become more widely available and more popular, their price also has moderated to bring them into competition with other popular houseplants. The standards can grow quite large, twelve inches or more, and the miniatures or dwarfs are about half that size. Even the tiniest have a touch of elegance. Try placing a single dwarf white cyclamen in a small arrangement of greens. Try three large pinks or lavenders massed together—the effect is spectacular!

Cyclamens are not difficult, but they are particular. Their main requirement is to have cool, bordering on downright cold, temperatures. It will not do to let this plant sit in your heated living room even if the temperature drops ten degrees at night! Cyclamens want night temperatures in the forties or fifties and will thrive if given close to the same conditions during the day. They have not forgotten their ancient origins in the mountains of Iran where many still grow wild. There, the nights are cold and the days are cool.

Last winter I kept a healthy and beautiful cyclamen in our garage, which is heated to forty degrees. Admittedly the plant sat in front of a window where the sun warmed it up a bit during the day, but not nearly to the same temperature as in our living room. Frequent visits inside to be admired did it no harm at all! It bloomed profusely all winter, and in March it went off to compete in our regional spring flower show.

Second only to cool temperatures is the cyclamen's requirement for water. They are heavy drinkers and want their soil to be constantly moist. Add a little fertilizer twice a month. Water them around the edge of the pot being careful not to pour water on the corm, the fleshy "bulb" from which the leaves and flower stems grow. Not a true bulb, the corm actually is an enlarged section of stem that has swollen up to hold nutrients that will be expended as the plant takes up its food during its growth cycle. New corms will be formed from buds next to the old corm.

Cyclamen

Care of the corm is critical in keeping the cyclamen through the summer and bringing it into bloom a second or even a third time. Removal of the spent flowers and leaves should be done as they wilt. A nurseryman once showed me how to do this—by gently twirling or twisting the stem until it pulls loose from the corm with a slight tug. Yanking the stem out can damage the outside skin of the corm and, for some reason, is also detrimental to new growth the following season.

Once the plant stops blooming and the leaves begin to yellow, put it aside and stop watering. It will be a dreadful mess, but never mind. Remove the old foliage as it dies off, and allow the soil to dry out completely. At this point, you can repot it in a pot that is one size larger using a commercial potting soil mix. Do not place the corm any deeper than it was before. As the plant ages, you will find that the corm gets larger and is placed higher in the pot. It may end up halfway above the soil line if you do a good job! Place the new pot in the shade outdoors, keep it moderately moist through the summer and watch for new growth to emerge.

In all honesty, I have not had very good luck with this process. It's worth trying as an experiment, but my second-year cyclamens have been pale imitations of their former selves. One of these days, or years, I might learn something more, and it just might work! In the meantime, I've gotten over the guilt of tossing out the old one to make room for the next new elegant beauty!

Shaping for Show

As I bring in the houseplants for another winter season, I am taking a hard and fond look at some old favorites: an ugly schefflera badly in need of pruning, ivy trained on a hoop but now running away, a pittosporum running wild. These are family members, tried and true. Keepers.

Even the keepers need a reassessment after having spent the summer outdoors, and this is the time. If your indoor space is limited, as mine is, you don't want to devote it to plants that are not up to par or don't look their best for whatever reason. Why put up with an ugly plant unless you have some particular sentimental attachment to it? And if it looks ugly to you, its parent, think what it will look like to other people! Treat yourself to the best. Although the first rule is cleanliness, there is no point in washing and spraying a plant, or repotting it, unless that plant is as close to its best as you can make it. Think of this plant as a person, wanting to shine for a special event, the high school prom, a wedding, or holiday party. Then put yourself in that plant's position as an entry for a flower show, as a prized gift, as the focal point of your interior under lights. Think perfection! Think pruning!

The key words here are time, sharp, and judgment. Take time before making any cuts. Once they're made, that's it. You can't put the stem back on the trunk.

Arm yourself with the sharpest clippers you have. It's worth having them sharpened for the occasion if they have grown dull. Clean cuts are healthy cuts and will heal well, but if a stem is torn or smashed, the plant's tissue will be damaged and will be very susceptible to disease. Fill a little cup with rubbing alcohol, and dip the clippers in it for each cut you make. This will help prevent the spread of disease, especially when you move from one plant to another.

Along with the time you'll take, apply your best judgment about shape, form, and aesthetics. You should have a finished product that looks the way you want it to.

Begin by looking for any blemishes or worse! Leaves that are torn, have holes for whatever reason, are badly yellowed, or have brown tips are not going to come back to be healthy green leaves again. Get rid of them now by cutting them off at the base of their petioles, or little stems. Then stand back and consider what you have left.

Now is the time to look at the overall form of the plant. If you have had to cut off a good many leaves, you may have to reshape the plant. If it is a fairly large member of the dracaena family, a dieffenbachia, or one of the large philodendrons, its stems are growing up from the center of the plant. To reduce its size, cut off one or two of the largest stems or trunks at the level of the soil to allow the smaller and younger stems to take over. Then, remaining true to the form of the plant as it is meant to be, trim the smaller branches and twigs above to create the proportion and shape you want. In the case of my schefflera, uneven growth had occurred during the summer as I had neglected to rotate it toward the light as often as I should have. I pruned off several of the longer twiggy stems, which were ungainly and crossing against each other, and opened up the center of the plant to admit more light and air circulation.

Remember that wherever you make a cut new growth will occur. You don't want to turn the center stem of your plant into a head with two horns going off at opposite angles! It's better to make cuts down in the center of the plant where the new growth won't have a jarring appearance, at least not to begin with. Make your cuts just above the nodes, the places on the stem from which new leaves grow, and where the new growth cells are most active.

Trimming my runaway ivy hoop presents a different challenge. Again, I look for any yellowing leaves, spindly stems that are not carrying their fair share of leaves, and uneven bunching up—places where the growth is disproportionately thick or where a spindly stem mars the shape of the trained plant. A lot of this trimming and clipping is personal choice. Go for the look you like. Again, remember that new growth will occur from a cut. Two or more new little stems will emerge, so plan ahead.

When your plants are in shape, get on with the cleaning and spraying task. A good hard spray under the garden hose is the best first step. Then allow the foliage to dry, and give it the first application of insecticide, meticulously following the directions for use. Protect your skin and eyes with a scarf and glasses. I usually tie a scarf over my nose and mouth.

Be sure to spray the top of the potting medium where little larvae and eggs can lurk under the debris of fallen leaves and twigs. After going through this cycle once, I spray again a few days later just to be certain that I am not carrying any unwanted creatures inside my house.

Don't forget to scrutinize your pots as carefully as the plants. Give them a good scrubbing. They and the plants go to the prom together!

Fussing Over African Violets

Aﬁcan violets are the perfect choice for a fussbudget. The key to keeping them happy is in the details, and the proper details are all it takes. The *Saintpaulia*'s reputation as the favorite plant of little old ladies is totally deserved. This is a perfect example of mutualism, in which two species support each other in a cozy and caring environment.

What is good for little old ladies is good for African violets. They like warm temperatures. They do not care for strong sunlight, but will take a bit of it through a window in the winter. They prefer a warm bath to a shower, with the emphasis on warm or tepid, neither hot nor cold. They do not like to have wet heads. They do not like to have chilly bedrooms. They do not like sitting in a draft. What do they like?

They like to eat and drink sparingly, and only a little at a time. They like to be cozy, all tucked into their pots. They like plenty of light, preferably from overhead. They do like attention and will respond generously when given the TLC they crave!

Little old men grow African violets, too. In fact, the African Violet Society of America has a huge membership of all ages to exchange information and register new hybrids. The *Saintpaulia* is one of the world's most popular flowering houseplants and, once its growing conditions are understood and met, one of the most rewarding.

From just a few natural species, growers have developed thousands of hybrids with characteristics ranging from different shapes of leaves, smooth or fuzzy, to a variety of flower shapes in singles and doubles. The most commonly grown African violet is easy for the amateur to recognize. Its leaves grow outward from the center of the plant in a circular pattern to form a rosette that lies flat. Small five-lobed flowers grow in the shape of a small, rounded dome in the center of the rosette or pop up randomly on short stems here and there among the leaves, giving the plant a less formal and decidedly impish appearance. Blossoms come in shades of blue, purple, lavender, white, and pink. Some have ruffled borders of different shades or totally different colors. Some of the leaves are variegated as well. Some African violets are trailing, with their flowers tumbling here and there on long tendrils.

As with every houseplant, the *Saintpaulia's* origins give us the clues we need to care properly for it. The *Saintpaulias* are not violets at all, but gesneriads. They originate in East Africa in a small area covering southern Kenya and coastal Tanzania. Their natural habitat is warm, shaded, and moist. They like daytime temperatures of seventy to seventy-five degrees, with a slight drop at night to sixty-five and no lower than sixty.

Bright light, a north or east exposure, is the best. They thrive under artificial lights. We find them for sale, looking delightfully content in garden centers under grow lights, where the light intensity is constant and where the plants' distance from the light source can be controlled. They do best placed about six inches under cool fluorescent or grow lights. (Remember that the strongest light intensity is under the center of the tube.) In that way, the leaves will maintain their spreading habit and the flower stems will stay short and not get leggy reaching for light.

African Violet

Proper watering is another key to success. The delicate root systems of these plants should never dry out and must be kept moist with watering on demand. The fussbudget must check them every day, poking into the soil with a finger to be sure that they are not totally dry. The fussbudget must be sure that the water is tepid and that no water gets splashed on the leaves or, if it does, gets wiped off immediately with a paper towel. Cold water absorbed through the root system may cause permanent white spots or a white web-like condition on the leaves.

Some fussbudgets bottom water by placing the pot in a saucer of tepid water and allowing the soil to absorb it through the holes in the bottom of the pot. This is OK but not necessary. Feed once or twice a month, using a half-strength balanced fertilizer (20-20-20) or one of the African violet plant fertilizers. Watch carefully to monitor any sign of crustiness around the edge of the pot and/or across the surface of the soil. This would be the residue or build up of excess salts from the fertilizer and could be harmful to the stems of the plants. If this occurs, water heavily with plain tepid water, and allow it to drain through the pot several times over a few weeks to flush out the residue and clean the growing medium.

African violets are easily propagated by leaf cuttings. Prepare a rooting medium of moist sand (not beach sand) or vermiculite or whatever you like to use. Reach into the center of the plant and snap off a medium-sized middle-aged leaf, neither the oldest nor the youngest, as cleanly as possible. If any bit of that petiole, or stem, is left at the base of the parent plant, cut it off to prevent rotting. Cut off all but about one inch of the petiole, make a hole in the medium about half an inch deep with a pencil, and insert the cutting into it. Using a fresh hormone rooting powder such as Rootone will greatly aid this process. Just follow the directions on the package, but be aware that these products have a shelf life.

Keep the medium moist, and watch for the new little plants to emerge. When the new leaves are just shy of an inch long, pry them up, rinse off the roots, and pot them up in African violet soil. Pretty soon, you'll be fussing over an entire collection!

Divide, Conquer, and Multiply

We've done our job too well! Now we have plants so vigorous and healthy that they are pushing the limits of their pots. You can tell that a plant is pot-bound when the roots start to climb up, out, and over the rim of the pot or when the pot begins to crack open from the inside out. Another sign is that there's no soil surface left to absorb water and not enough soil to supply nutrients. What to do?

Pot-bound plants are candidates for a process known as root division. This is just what it sounds like—dividing the roots of a plant into sections, or pieces, to relieve its misery and create more plants at the same time. Think of every root section as a potential plant, and you will easily see that intertwined roots can be separated and repotted to produce new plants. While this is only one form of propagation, sometimes it is the only way to go.

Tackling a division for the first time takes courage, but it is a great learning experience. The first thing to do is to get over your reverence for the root. It is only one part of the plant, although arguably the most important one. It is tougher than you think and will take poking, prodding, and even cutting if need be. The second thing to do is to recognize that if you don't do something, the plant will languish and perhaps die. So what have you got to lose?

Not every plant is a candidate for this process. The first consideration is the health of the plant. If you were facing surgery, you'd want to be in the best possible condition to withstand it. Division is a shock to the system and is best overcome if the plant is healthy to begin with and has the opportunity to recuperate in optimum surroundings. Spring is a good time to divide. Warm, fresh air in shady conditions will provide the plant with the best chance for its roots and foliage to recuperate and go on to have a good shot at recovery.

Making the basic decision, to divide or not, is largely a matter of common sense along with understanding how the plant grows. For anything to be divisible there must be more than one of it—otherwise we're talking about "la guillotine!" Fortunately, multiples exist in various forms—numerous stems and lots of eyes on a tuber, for example.

Plants that have several stems growing up from the base or soft new stem growth at the soil level are ideal. Examples are the Boston ferns, spathiphyllum, Swedish ivies, asparagus ferns, and some of the dieffenbachias. Plants that send out little plantlets or offsets are divisible. In short, if you see a lot of soft growth spreading around the surface of the soil in the pot, or tiny reproductions of the parent plant, you can probably divide it.

What cannot be divided? A single stemmed plant, especially one with woody bark. Even if you see a lot of side stems, look carefully at the base of the plant for a single stem or small trunk. Also, trailing and climbing plants cannot be divided, but you don't need to worry about them. They can be cut back easily to manageable levels. Succulents such as the Christmas cactus and jades cannot be divided.

Rhizomes and tubers can be divided so long as each piece keeps one or more eyes, but that's another story!

If you are dividing for the first time, try a small-sized plant that will not present too daunting a problem, perhaps an African violet or a small Swedish ivy. Have all your materials ready in advance, so that you won't keep the roots exposed for too long and allow them to get too dry. You will need two or three new pots the correct size for the divisions—about two inches larger than the new little root balls will be. Eyeball the sizes ahead of time. Have the pots ready, clean, and crocked. Have your potting soil mixed and ready. Have on hand a little dish of alcohol, some bamboo or metal skewers, and a sharp knife. Plastic chopsticks used in Chinese restaurants are super tools for gently probing and separating root masses.

Prepare some wet paper towels and plastic baggies in case you have to hold the new divisions aside before they can get potted up. Once you begin, work as quickly as possible.

Knock the plant out of its pot, and shake off the excess soil. Small little plantlets might naturally fall apart, but if they are compacted hard together, soaking the root mass might help. Pry the roots apart with your fingers, or use a chopstick or skewer to gently separate the roots. Pot up the new divisions, maintaining the same soil level in their new pots as they had previously. Keep two or three divisions together if they are very small. Water them lightly and place them out of direct sunlight until they are recovered and showing growth.

In the case of a tightly pot-bound plant, such as an overgrown asparagus fern, you might have to divide the root ball by cutting it with a knife. Be sure that the knife is very sharp and sterilized with alcohol. Trim the foliage down close to the soil level, lay the plant on its side, and cut straight through the root mass, dividing the whole business in half or thirds. Try to maintain the existing proportion of root ball to stems and foliage. Once the root ball is opened up, you might find that the center core is old and weak, in which case cut it out. Pot up the divisions as above.

Now, wasn't that easy? You've conquered division, and multiplied your collection. This may become a habit, especially with your gift list in mind!

Agave—A Theatrical Native American

The Sonoran Desert of southern Arizona is a living laboratory for the study of several plant families that share the characteristics that have enabled them to survive. Hundreds of years ago, human families sustained themselves in this desert using only native plants and animals as sources for food, clothing, and shelter. Although necessity was the mother of invention, our ancestors must have been creative risk-takers.

One of the best examples of an all-purpose resource is the Agave family, truly remarkable plants in any era. The agave's dramatic looks, its romantic history, and its usefulness to early desert peoples, as well as its economic significance today, make it one of the most important of the succulent plants. It has gained acceptance as a container plant in all climates and makes a colorful statement as the focus of an indoor garden room or an outdoor patio.

There is a large body of legend surrounding the agave, beginning with its name, which in Greek means "noble" or "illustrious." There does not seem to be any relationship between the plant and the Agave of myth, unless it is the pulque connection. Agave was a figure in Greek mythology who killed her son while drunk under a spell inflicted upon the women of Thebes by Dionysius. Her story might relate to the plant only as it was later used in the rites of human sacrifice practiced by the Aztecs. The juice of the agave plant, when fermented, was called pulque and was highly intoxicating. It was widely used by the Aztecs, especially in their religious ceremonies when they would drink huge quantities of pulque before cutting up their human victims and roasting them alive. On the other hand, with good intentions and before anyone knew about fetal alcohol syndrome, they gave it to pregnant women and nursing mothers because of its nutritional value!

The natives used every bit of the plant for food, clothing, and shelter. The agaves moved northward with Native Americans and across to Europe and other Spanish colonies to be used as ornamentals and for economic and medicinal purposes. The plant still is widely used as a source of fiber, sisal, and hemp, and of course, to make mescal and tequila.

It's very nice to be able to study a plant that truly is a native American as so many of our houseplants have been bred from exotics originating in Asia or Africa. This is a desert plant that, over the centuries, has learned how to use its body parts to perform the basic functions of life. Living in areas of extreme heat and cold, having to get anchored and take nourishment in dry gritty soils, and putting up with drought or deluge, these plants have thought it through and have been successful!

The agave is a succulent, storing water in thick, fleshy leaves that can shrivel or expand or drop off as necessary. It grows in the form of a rosette with almost no stem between the leaves and the soil to reduce moisture loss. Each leaf is wide at the common base and ends in a point from which a thorn emerges. Some species have thorns along the margins of the leaves all the way from base to tip. They vary in size from quite small to fourteen or fifteen feet in diameter, and their leaves vary in color from a blue green to gray green, or the colors can be variegated.

When the rosette is mature, which can happen in just a few years for the smaller varieties, but can take forty or fifty years for the larger ones, it sends up a tall flower spike. Often called the Century Plant for its once-in-a-while blossom, a large agave puts on quite a show when the time comes. The flower stalk grows fast, often measured at an inch or more per day and can attain heights of twenty to thirty feet. Little branch-like limbs or arms bearing the yellow or white flowers grow out at right angles from the main stem that, by this time, looks like a small tree trunk. Frankly, this is not an attractive plant part, being more fascinating and theatrical

46

than beautiful, but a desert hillside of them in bloom is eye-catching to say the least! Once it has put all of its energy and nutrients into the flower stalk, the parent dies off, but not before sending out its pups, or offsets, at the base of the rosette.

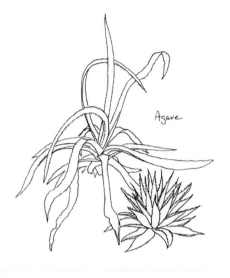

Agave

As with all plants, understanding the agave's needs in its native habitat provides the best clues for care. They prefer a sunny window with cool temperatures during the winter months, as cool as possible at night, and your average house temperature during the day. Withhold water during January and February, or give them only enough to prevent them from shriveling. Water a bit more as you get into the spring months, when their period of active growth occurs, but allow the soil to dry out between waterings. They like to be sprayed with a light mist—they'll think that they're back in the desert!

They can summer outdoors in a dry spot but not direct sun at first. Water sparingly from summer until December when they once again go into their dry and dormant period. If you decide to pot up the pups, allow them to sit out in the open a day or two to allow the small roots to form calluses before placing them in their new pots. Add plenty of drainage to the bottom of the new containers and pat the soil down firmly around the new little plants. Withhold water for about a week.

Be prepared to stand back if your agave starts to bloom, and call the neighbors in!

Dusting Off the Veltheimia

M y *Veltheimia* bulbs have survived a summer of tough love. Once again, as I bring them indoors for the winter, I marvel at their life cycle. Dusting them off, yes literally, I cannot see any evidence that within a few months they will be sending forth their ruffled leaves and thrusting their flower stalks upward. But they will, as surely as God's little green apples soon will cover the orchard floor.

The tough love part goes back to my own learning experience with these bulbs. Years ago, a friend gave me two tiny bulblets, explaining that she didn't really want any more of this particular plant, and said, "Just pot them up, dear, and you'll be surprised."

As I had never heard of the bulb, she spelled the name for me. Dutifully, I cared for them and, for the first few years, they survived but didn't especially thrive. They did not grow any larger, put out a few weak green leaves in the spring, and that was about it. My next exposure to this plant came when visiting a botanical garden where I encountered two large specimens potted up, lying on their sides outdoors in a broiling hot sun in the middle of the summer. Although not identifiable except as bulbs, I was told that they were veltheimias.

"That's how they like it all summer, dear," explained their caretaker. "Makes them think they're back in South Africa, hot as blazes!"

And so, ever since, in the name of tough love I take my veltheimia pots outdoors in June, lay them down where chipmunks cannot reach them

Veltheimia

and where full sunlight will hit them, if there is to be sunlight, and forget about them until fall. Then I dust them off to remove the remnants of pollen, dust, and debris that have collected on their wrinkled white skins, knock off the top layer of old soil, add some fresh topsoil, and begin to water them again. Regular feedings can begin once the first green shoot appears. My bulbs never fail to leaf out shortly after re-entry and flower around January.

This plant should be more popular than it is, and I suppose that it is just one of those plants that enjoy popularity in cycles. It has proven to be tough, as you can see from my encounters with it, dependable, and remarkably pest-free, especially when indoors. And, by the way, it is beautiful!

A member of the family Hyacinthaceae, veltheimia blossoms follow the same pattern on the stem as the little hyacinth florets and as muscari, both members of this same family. Many species that formerly sported names of their own are now identified simply as either *V. bracteata* or *V. capensis*. The many common names include Forest Lily, Cape Lily, and Winter Red-Hot Poker. The last may be a bit misleading, as it is not really red but can be a hot pink. The inflorescence is dense atop a sturdy stalk that does not require staking, although it will bend toward the light source. The many flowers are tubular, reaching outward at the top and gradually bending downward around the top of the stem.

My flowers are a pale pink color, with a touch of blue green at their tips. Colors can range from this pale pink to orange, pink, or deep rose. There is a form that sports reddish purple flowers and has longer and narrower foliage. The foliage of these plants is attractive enough to stand on its own, even without the flower stalk. The green is bright and fresh, the surface shines naturally, and the margins of the large outwardly-spreading leaves are gently ruffled.

Veltheimias like bright light, and even a few hours of direct sunlight, but once they begin to flower they should stay out of the sun. As mentioned above, the flower stalk will bend readily to the source of light, so the plant should be rotated frequently. The soil should be kept moist, and the bulb will benefit from a light feeding with balanced fertilizer (20-20-20) once or twice a month. Once the flower fades, cut off the flower stalk and maintain the foliage with regular feedings and waterings until it changes color in the late spring. It is then once again time for the tough love treatment.

When the bulb puts out offsets, break them off gently and pot them up separately. This is best done in the fall when the newly potted pups will receive optimum care. Veltheimias can be grown from seed, but it might be a lengthy process.

If you are interested in a veltheimia, one of your biggest challenges might be to find one. Several of the most popular bulb catalogs do not even list veltheimia. If, after checking with local garden centers you come up empty, try online at telosrarebulbs.com, which did have two varieties available when I checked it out. Another site to try is diggingdog.com, although the last time I tried there, they were sold out—which ought to send a message!

If we create the demand, the supply might follow. It's worth a try, dear.

3

In the Comfort Zone

Spider Plants for Fun and Smiles

There's something about a spider plant that makes you smile!
Maybe it is the likeness to a real spider, a tiny center surrounded by long, skinny "legs" that go out in all directions. Maybe it is the plant's blatant craving to reproduce itself, creating its tiny offspring on the long "umbilical cord" runners that dangle from the parent plant. Maybe it is just the joy that is provided by an attractive plant in healthy condition. But therein lies the problem.

It's the healthy condition that is easier to hope for than to attain.

Although described as one of the easiest plants to grow and a good plant for beginners, in fact *Chlorophytum comosum* is somewhat challenging. My two spider plants that are about to come indoors are definitely the worse for wear after their summer under my deck. Mea culpa! I was not as vigilant as I should have been with regular watering during the dog days of July and August. But other plants have come through just fine. Proper watering is the key to good spider plant care.

A healthy spider plant has vigorous, long, grassy leaves that are totally green or variegated. But all too often, the tips of these leaves are brown, which detracts from the overall beauty of the plant. The generally accepted theory about this browning is that it is caused by the presence of fluoride, sodium salts, and/or chlorine in tap water. Most people don't care—they just live with it.

But now that I feel guilty about these plants, I'm going to care and see if I can avoid this leaf-tip browning problem. The best way is to collect rain water and use it to water the plants, or to use distilled water. Keep the soil constantly moist, but not soggy, and do not let it dry out between waterings.

Leaf browning can also be caused by direct sunlight on the leaves and can be avoided by keeping the plants in bright light but not sunlight. They like humidity and a drop in nighttime temperatures. They like only an occasional feeding with half strength balanced fertilizer (20-20-20). They do not like to sit or hang in a draft.

Mention hanging, and this plant is the first to come to mind. Its runners droop away from the center of the plant and can't wait to produce offspring, the little spiderettes, or plantlets, or spiderlets, or whatever we like to call them. A good-sized parent plant with loads of little spiderlets hanging from it is, in fact, a spectacular show. It's only a short wait for the children to have grandchildren, and on it goes with many generations dangling from each other and living out of the same pot. The fun, of course, is in removing the spiderlets and rooting them up to go off on their own.

The plants are most apt to reproduce in the fall when the days get shorter, so be watchful. The most foolproof way to root up a spiderlet is

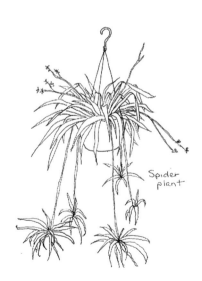

Spider plant

to place it, while still attached to its mother, on a small pot of loose potting medium and secure it in place with a hairpin or opened paper clip, or lightly tie it to a small stake. Keep the medium moist and the baby will quickly take root. Once this happens, cut it away from its "umbilical cord" runner, and it is on its own. Or, cut the plantlet loose leaving most of the runner attached to it, and pot it up as above. Two little plantlets could be done at the same time, keeping the runner between them until roots form. Then cut away the runner.

Another, but less satisfactory, method is to cut the baby away from the main plant, place it in a cup of water keeping its bottom moist until roots begin to form, and then pot it up in soil. Be aware that roots formed in water do not always survive or do well when moved into soil, so the first method is definitely the better one.

Obviously, hanging your spider plant is the best way to display it. Placing it up on an old-fashioned Victorian plant stand is also effective, especially if you leave the spiderlets in place.

Several cultivars of *Chlorophytum comosum* are available, but Vittatum is the most common. It has pale green leaves, four to eight inches long, with a white central stripe. There is a dwarf, Mandaianum, with shorter leaves and a yellow stripe. Variegatum has very long leaves that are about an inch wide with white edges.

A side benefit of having spider plants in your home may be their ability to help maintain good air quality. A joint study completed in 1989 by NASA and the Associated Landscape Contractors of America suggested that common houseplants may help reduce indoor pollution by absorbing toxins from the air. The principal researcher in that study was NASA scientist Dr. Bill Wolverton, who has authored several books including *How to Grow Fresh Air,* Penguin Group USA, 1997. Of the plants tested, the spider plant came out as one of the best performers, reducing highly toxic levels of carbon dioxide to nontoxic levels in just twenty-four hours.

One spider plant may not make that much difference, but think of all those children and grandchildren going to work for you!

Putting Up With Mother-in-Law's Tongue

Whenever a family reunion or event looms, we look forward to renewing our ties...or do we? Dare we admit that one particular relative must be reckoned with yet again? Yes, it's the mother-in-law!

How and why such a stereotype got established is not clear, but established it is. I had one, and now I am one. Sooner or later, most mothers will be in this position, carrying a name that suggests negative and unpleasant characteristics, whether or not they are deserved. Maybe the name is part of the problem.

The same is true in the plant world. The common names of plants usually describe certain characteristics, most often related to the plants' flowers. Examples of good names are the Shrimp plant with its coral, curved flowers, the Lipstick plant with its bright red, openmouthed flowers, and others like the Silver Dollar Tree, the String of Beads, the Powder Puff plant, and on and on. It is easy to see how plants like these got their common names, but it's also easy to see how they could acquire more than one name that is equally descriptive. An example of this is *Rhoeo discolor* which has various common names like Moses in a Cradle or Man in a Boat that describe the shape of the plant's flower. Another example is the Chenille plant, *Acalypha hispida*, which also is called Red Hot Cat Tail, describing its bright red, fuzzy inflorescence.

This is why botanists use the botanical names of plants to avoid confusion and provide absolute identification. As we'll see, when common names are applied, mistakes get made. But the common names are easier to remember and use and have a lot to do with our attitude toward the plant.

Question: Would you want a Mother-in-Law's Tongue in your living room? See answer below!

Taking a good look at the *Sansevieria*, it's easy to figure out how it got its unfortunate but amusing common name. Assuming that the name was adopted in jest by a botanist, or applied to the plant by someone who really hated his/her mother-in-law, it fits either way.

The succulent leaves are large and long, like tongues thrusting up from the base of the plant. Although I consider my plant quite handsome, with its cross-striping pattern of a darker green against a lighter background, it does dominate the group of plants arranged around it. The margins of the leaves are yellow bands with very cutting edges, and the point of the tongue-like leaf is sharp enough to be a weapon of minor destruction.

It is a tough plant, able to withstand a lot of adverse conditions that would kill something more tender, although it does not like to be chilly. It grows slowly. It is tenacious, hanging around for a long time in its pot without asking for different quarters.

Another common name for *Sansevieria* is Snake plant, probably for the wavy, cross-striping pattern in the leaves.

This plant is an example of how common names can be confusing and lead to incorrect identification. There is a dieffenbachia also called Mother-in-Law's Tongue because of a compound in the leaves. When the leaves are chewed, as they probably once were by the natives of Costa Rica where the plant originated, this compound causes the chewer to become temporarily speechless and to have a very painful tongue and mouth for a while. This dieffenbachia is also called Dumb Cane for the same reason. I don't know whether this means that a mother-in-law renders her children speechless by dominating the conversation herself, or simply that she is painful to be around. Either way, the name fits again!

All kidding aside, *Sansevieria* is a super houseplant. The average indoor home temperature will suit it fine, but it does not like night temperatures below sixty-five degrees. Since it is a succulent, water it generously but seldom, especially in the winter. Mature plants should be fed occasionally from early spring through the fall, but not in the winter.

Eventually, when the plant puts out enough offsets to crowd its pot, or when you notice that the leaves are not as healthy as they should be, it is time to divide it. Use root division, especially for *Sansevieria laurentii*, in order to perpetuate the yellow margin along the leaf edge. See "Divide, Conquer, and Multiply" in this book, or refer to a good houseplant guide for the correct technique of root division. Place each new division in a clean,

Mother-in-law tongue

crocked pot large enough to hold the new root ball. Set the divisions as deep as they were in their old pot. *Sansevierias* like a little extra superphosphate and a bit of ground limestone. Water the new plants generously, and drain them well. Let a few weeks go by before you start to feed them.

So, the answer to the above question is a resounding YES! These plants are great to live with.

You can talk to your Mother-in-Law's Tongue, and it won't talk back. It won't give you any problems while serving as an attractive and decorative home companion. It will not be demanding, will require very little tending, and will respond to your occasional ministrations with a good performance. If and when it doesn't do any of these things, or you get tired of having it around, you can just throw it out!

Gonna Let My Little Light Shine

One of the features I like best about our contemporary home is the lighting. Its track lighting is, for the most part, a dramatic and welcome change from the little antique table lamps of the traditional houses in my previous life. We switch on our happy lights for breakfast early on winter mornings and again in the late afternoon hours. They are cheerful, they light up art on the walls, they shine down on our reading chairs, and they give a glow to the entire interior.

Thinking of plants as people, we provide happy lights for them as well. I can tell by the plants' general health and performance during winter months that they are kept as happy as we are. The leaves are a bright and shiny green, the foliage is compact, and orchids and gesneriads bloom for long periods.

The reason that I have been able to garden under lights for many years is that I have a handy husband. Without his assistance, I would have been scared off by articles and books about light gardening. Terms like footcandles, incandescent vs. fluorescent tubes, ultraviolet light, and the spectrum are enough to terrify any nontechie like me! But with his help, and after years of doing it, I can promise you that it is easy, nonthreatening, not complicated, and extremely rewarding. Furthermore, once a setup is established, the plants are easier to maintain than they would be without the lights!

The advantages are many:

- The plants have a constant and dependable set of conditions that never vary. Therefore, sunny vs. cloudy days are irrelevant.
- With several plants in one location under lights, much less maintenance is required. Humidity and air circulation can be provided for all of them together, and there is no need to move them around.
- One can grow certain species that would not do well in a normal home setting in the winter. In particular, orchids like *Paphiopedilum* and *Phalaenopsis* will thrive under lights, as will most of the gesneriads. African violets love them.
- You can make use of "dead space" in your home where nothing else is going on—an unused closet, a section of the basement, or an inside wall in need of attention.
- A light garden is beautiful—it adds enormously to your décor!

The disadvantages are few:

- The principal disadvantage is a slightly higher electric bill, but it's not that bad with the use of fluorescent tubes, as we will see.
- Some very large houseplants might be difficult to fit under a light, but I have solved that by designating a section of a room as a light garden and using ceiling track lighting. It is difficult to find all-in-one light garden units (e.g., tables or benches) that have the light fixtures in place and are all ready to go. I found two of mine at a yard sale. Some styles may be available at flower shows, in garden centers, and through nursery catalogs, but they tend to be expensive. Therefore, the challenge is to do it yourself.

Now it's time to get it together. Select the area in your home for a light garden, remembering that you will need to allow space for more than the lights. The plants should be placed on trays filled with pebbles or aggregate to provide a steady source of humidity, and there should be space for a small fan to keep the air moving. And, of course, the obvious, there should be an outlet or two nearby. Plan the space with sizes of tubes in mind. Fluorescent tubes come in lengths of two feet, four feet, and eight

feet. The eight-footer is the most efficient, but not everyone has this much space. The four-footer is good. The two-footer is barely adequate, although it happens that my two little freestanding units take two-foot tubes. They are not very energy efficient, but they're what I've got, they're kind of cute, and I squeeze a lot into the space.

Speaking of energy, it's time to talk tubes. I have never used anything except fluorescent tubes, two side by side, one cool white and one warm white. A horticulturist friend and true expert, who has been winning prizes for years with her plants grown under lights, uses exactly the same combination. You don't need all those tubes sold under special names suggesting proper horticulture! The combination of cool white and warm white fluorescent tubes will give you exactly the same results for a fraction of the cost. Their efficiency in use of electricity and distribution of light is also much higher than incandescent bulbs.

Fluorescent tubes are sold in pairs in fixtures that have a reflector hood, often with chains attached, ready for mounting or hanging. They are easily found in the lighting departments of large home stores. Any style is fine as long as it provides two tubes side by side. Shorter lengths may be found for mounting under a kitchen cabinet or within a frame of your own design.

In planning your growing area, remember that the strongest light is emitted from the center of the tube and grows weaker out toward the ends. You can place high-light plants and low-light plants accordingly. Plants will reach for light, so you want to keep the lights no more than four to six inches above the plants to prevent leggy, spindly growth. There are huge advantages to growing seedlings under lights. They can be kept under totally controlled conditions, thus preparing them for the shock of going outdoors!

Putting the lights on a timer is another step in a low-maintenance routine. My plants under lights get up at 7:00 AM and go to sleep at 9:00 PM, and length of days can be adjusted depending on species or special projects. And you can go away during the winter with a light heart ... Sorry, I couldn't resist!

A Hoya Makes Sweet Scents

As I move my *Hoya carnosa* outdoors for its twenty-fifth summer, I once again marvel at my good fortune in having this plant. Its silver anniversary is the perfect occasion to toot its horn! I call this my 5-L plant, excelling in longevity, loyal performance, and lush blooms and all on a low-maintenance routine. Lucky me!

It all began with a move into a new home many years ago when a friend arrived with this plant as a housewarming present. It was young but full and luxuriant, filling out its hanging pot but not yet growing its characteristic long tendrils. The friend was so enthusiastic about this plant and its blossoms that I immediately hung it in a place of honor and waited for it to bloom, and waited, and waited...

Then I made a big mistake. Not leaving well enough alone, I decided to prune back the long, skinny tendrils called spurs that were becoming too long and out of proportion to the bushy shape of the plant. Too late, I learned that these spurs are required for the plant to bloom, as the flowers grow directly from them unaccompanied by foliage—an unconventional arrangement to say the least. I paid for my impetuous pruning with a few more years of waiting for those spurs to grow back, which they finally did to a length of two feet and longer. Small wonder that the flowers were treasures when they finally emerged!

When they bloom the flowers last for a long time, filling the air with a unique pungency. The hoya is a succulent, storing water in its leathery leaves for long periods of time. The flowers also have a succulent look as they are thick and fleshy, although tiny, within an inflorescence rich in detail. Their smooth shiny surface and almost artificial look give the plant another name, Porcelain Flower. The flowers, borne in clusters, are a masterpiece of design detail. Each tiny flower is supported by a slim red stem. Each flower looks like a pale pink five-pointed star that is topped by another five-pointed star in white, centered with red. When in bloom, and especially in dry weather, droplets of nectar hang directly on each tiny little yellow center making the clusters glisten and sparkle with their sweet-scented moisture.

Hoya

In the summer, my hoya hangs outside our front door in the shade, its spurs loaded with blossoms. I have counted twenty-four flower clusters within a two-week period!

Hoya carnosa is a member of the Asclepiadaceae family, native to eastern Asia and Australia. It also is called the Wax plant for the wax-like texture of the flowers and leaves. Another variety is *H.c.* 'Krinkle Kurl,' a.k.a. the Hindu Rope plant, which is smaller than *H. carnosa* and has tightly curled leaves on shorter stems. There are a few other varieties including 'Variegata,' whose leaves are edged with pink and/or white. All belong to one of the many families of succulents that originated in dry climates and, as a result, have learned to store water in their stems and leaves.

The camels of the plant world, succulents have a huge capacity for water storage that is to be drawn upon when the need arises. The hoyas are clearly stars among the succulents. In the twenty-five years that I have cared for my hoya, the guiding principle has been to leave it alone. In the winter, it hangs in a south-facing window that is situated under a porch overhang where it gets plenty of bright light but very little direct sunlight.

Leaves were scorched during one year when it spent the winter in direct sunlight, but new leaves grew in to replace them. It is fine with whatever indoor temperatures it receives, even down to fifty-five degrees if we go away for a while. It gets watered about once a month, but if we are away for longer it gets along fine. It gets fed maybe once in the early spring, and once again during its period of peak bloom. It does appreciate a rest or dormancy period after it blooms.

But this is the craziest part—it has been repotted only once in twenty-five years, and it seems to be severely pot-bound. If it were complaining, I would gladly repot it, but is producing twenty-four blossoms complaining? I don't think so.

If you must repot, use a soil mix with plenty of sand (not beach sand) or perlite for drainage. Keep the soil mix dry, put plenty of crocking in the bottom of the pot, and keep the roots near the surface when you place the plant in its new home. Contrary to standard procedure, do not water the newly repotted succulent for a few weeks after potting it up. Just spray the surface with a little mist to prevent the roots from drying out.

Hoyas are easily propagated by leaf cuttings, or woody stem cuttings, in moist sand. My plant seems to be growing from three separate stem sources, so perhaps it was originally three little plants in the same pot. Therefore, root division might be an option for me. But I'm not willing to pull it apart to find out!

Its untidy tendrils can be trained around a hoop or up a trellis while still performing their function as the "flower power" of the plant. Or, if you have space, let them swing and sway freely as I do, giving the plant a dramatic and somewhat wild profile. My guests have to dodge 'em when they come in the front door!

And now that you've done everything right, take time to smell the flowers!

Shamrock Wears the Green

Sweeping across fields and infiltrating woodlands in many parts of the world, they are ignored, taken for granted, or dug out as an invasive species. Potted up, they are adorable little plants, irresistible on florists' March display shelves. That shamrock you bought or were given for St. Patrick's Day is now to be reckoned with for what it really is ... and you will love it!

Most likely you and I have one of several species of *Oxalis*, also known as Wood Sorrel, which has found its way from Latin America into the nursery trade. In spite of confusion over taxonomy, which we'll only touch on here (aren't you glad!), this has been a good thing. Oxalis is amazingly adaptable as a houseplant, a cinch to grow, and bears a remarkable likeness to the real Irish shamrock. It may be said to be almost foolproof, a fact I can attest to from my own experience.

One of the first houseplants I acquired as a newlywed was an oxalis of average size, reasonably healthy, and, while not in bloom, of a good, bright green color. Not knowing anything about plants at the time, I plunked it down on a windowsill facing east, kept it fairly well watered, watched it bloom and then fade, half ignored it for a while, and then watched it grow, fill out and begin to put up tiny little stems ready to bud. In amazement I watched it burst into bloom again just in time for our local spring flower show in March. One of my friends was submitting some plants to the amateur section, grabbed my oxalis off the windowsill and took it in to submit with her plants. It won a blue ribbon, and I was hooked for life!

The oxalis sold in the United States as the shamrock probably is *O. montana,* a bulb plant that features delicate three-part leaves shaped like tiny rounded moths on slender stems—hence its substitution for the Irish shamrock. The flowers are in the form of tiny trumpets with five spiky petals, in white or pink, sometimes with narrow pink veins. *O. acetosella,* also fairly common in the trade, has four-part leaves and so, although it might bring good luck, this plant could not possibly be mistaken for the Irish shamrock if we are to believe the legend of St. Patrick.

Preaching to the ancient Irish, this missionary from England would reach down into the weeds at his feet, pluck a single clover with its three leaflets, and hold it up before the people as an illustration of the Christian Trinity—three in one. St. Patrick probably was holding onto a hop clover, *Medicago lupulina,* generally accepted as the original shamrock—the *seamróg* of Ireland. Earlier inhabitants of the Emerald Isle, the Druids, also held this plant as sacred because its leaves formed a triad, and three was a mystical number in the Druid religion.

Oxalis may not have been around as long as the *seamróg,* nor does it thrive in the cool, wet environs of the Emerald Isle! It is a tropical plant, which gives us clues about its care. It does best in full sun or very bright light, moderate humidity, and in a temperature range of fifty to seventy-five degrees. Water with tepid water, let it dry out a bit between waterings, and feed it a half-strength balanced fertilizer (20-20-20) every two weeks. Aphids may be attracted to it, so be on your guard. To prevent an infestation, keep good air circulation around these

Oxalis

plants, give them regular shower baths under the kitchen spray, and be prepared to take more drastic action if necessary.

Most of the species bear a strong resemblance to each other. *O. bowiei* bears flowers in rose and purple. *O. corymbosa* sends up eight- to twelve-inch leaves from the underground tuber and reproduces itself with tiny offsets. And *O. hirta* begins growth in an upright direction and then flops over, which makes it a good candidate for hangers and baskets.

Two species differ more noticeably from the others. *O. stricta* bears light yellow to reddish flowers, and its leaflets resemble clover. It favors drier soils in the eastern United States and is also native to Europe and parts of Asia. It is commonly called Indian Sorrel or Sheep's Clover. A dramatic houseplant is *O. purpurea* with its purple foliage and bright white and somewhat larger flowers. It blooms all during the winter months.

These little plants are so attractive that you might be tempted to use one or more of them as a centerpiece for a dinner party. If you do, you had better have plenty of candlelight. They are bright light plants and fold up their leaves in the dark as if they were praying!

Having bloomed for St. Pat, your oxalis deserves a rest. When the flowers start to fade and the foliage begins to yellow, stop feeding it and gradually give it less water. It can go outdoors in the summer if not allowed to dry out. In the fall, carefully tap it out of its pot and separate the small bulblets. You can repot them, a few together or as singles, in a general purpose potting soil or a mix of your choice that should include plenty of builders sand (not beach sand) or perlite and a bit of ground limestone. Resume watering and feeding as before. With the luck of the Irish, you should have several plants ready to give away in honor of St. Patrick on his next feast day!

Creating Clones

Cloning is not just for lab scientists looking for another Dolly or a biological breakthrough. Everyone who has ever cut off a piece of stem, rooted it, and grown it into a mature plant has done cloning. Also called taking cuttings, this procedure is simple and easy and gets results—lots of them!

Unlike a seed, which inherits its genetic material from parents and from previous generations, a cutting contains only the genetic material of the single parent plant from which it is cut. Taking cuttings is a process by which we pass on only specific genetic material to the next generation and ensure that the new plant's characteristics are exactly the same as its parent. No guesswork here!

Novices approach plant propagation as a learning experience. Experts see it as an opportunity to try new methods and discover new cultivars. With some professionals, it is a lucrative business, but it would be a very hard-hearted gardener who is not impressed and touched by the procedure of taking cuttings, also called slips. It is pretty amazing to be able to cut off part of a plant, perform some simple steps, and watch that part take root and become a whole and healthy, new plant. On this very elementary level, we can only imagine how Dolly's creator felt! At the least, it leaves me with a sense of awe about the power of the propagator, even though my lab is a bench under my deck and my equipment comes right out of the kitchen drawers!

There are stem cuttings and leaf cuttings. The procedures are a bit different, but the idea is the same. Following its natural instinct for survival, the cutting will want to stay alive and recreate the plant part that makes this possible, i.e., roots. We'll describe the procedure for taking stem cuttings but note that many species, such as African violets and begonias, are propagated more easily with leaf cuttings.

Early summer is a good time to take cuttings from many common houseplants as they put out new growth outdoors. The best results are achieved from stems grown in the current season and from a healthy plant in good condition. This is an opportunity to create plants for your entire holiday gift list that will cost you nothing except for the materials and labor!

You will need:

- a parent plant with plenty of stems to choose from
- small, individual plastic pots or six-pack flats or any container you can spare for a few weeks (fairly deep bowls, large salad bowls, plastic containers saved from take-out food, nonmetal casserole dishes)
- growing medium. I prefer builders sand (not beach sand), which can be obtained at any garden supply or landscape center because it stays firm and holds the newly emerging roots in place. Other choices include sterile potting soil mixed with perlite or vermiculite, or any seed-starting mix.
- a fresh package of hormone rooting powder, like Rootone, optional but advisable
- a very sharp razor blade or knife
- a small dish of alcohol
- a small dish of water
- a thin pencil or bamboo skewer
- plastic bags
- a mister filled with water
- plant labels, sticks, bamboo skewers, or anything that will hold the plastic bag up and away from the cutting once it is planted
- labels for the pots

From reading through the above list, you probably get the idea. Just line up the materials, string them together with some action verbs, and go to it!

Fill your container one-half to three-quarters with moistened sand. With a pencil, make a small hole in the sand to receive the cutting once it is ready. Find a stem on the plant that will give you a cutting about three to six inches long and that will retain at least two to three nodes. (A node is the point on the stem from which a leaf grows.) Dip the razor blade or knife into the alcohol, and make a sharp cut directly across, not diagonally, through the stem at a point just below one of the nodes. This ensures that the active growth cells at the node will be the ones called upon to create the new roots in the medium. Cut away any small stems or leaves near the base of the cutting. You can keep a few leaves near the top of the cutting but pinch off any flowers.

Moisten the bottom of the cutting with water and then dip it into the rooting powder. Tap off any excess powder, and place it gently into the hole you have made in the sand. Press the sand tightly around the cutting and mist it. If you want to place several cuttings in one large container be sure that they don't touch each other. Then place the whole thing in a plastic bag held up away from the cuttings with plant labels or sticks. Seal the bag tightly and label it or the container with the plant's name and date. You may think you'll remember, but you won't.

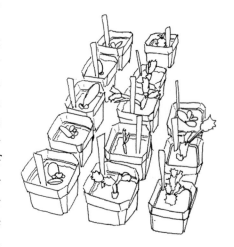

Keep the container in bright light, but not sunlight, at your average house temperature. If you can provide bottom heat with cables or a warm surface, things will go faster. The top of your refrigerator works well for this if there is enough light. Once every few days, remove the plastic cover to check on progress. Mist the planting medium if it is too dry, or remove the plastic cover for a few hours if too moist. What you are doing here is creating your own miniature greenhouse with its misting and heating systems!

It takes cuttings a few days or weeks to root, depending on the plant material. When the roots are well formed and about one inch long, transplant the cuttings into small individual pots filled with whatever medium is preferred by that species, and maintain them in bright light with good moisture until they are well established. Your well-grown roots are the key to success.

The most important part of this procedure is patience. Newly cloned plants, like Dolly, aren't made in a day!

4

Odd Fellows

Crown
of Thorns

Fooling Around with Stags

It all started with two tiny little ferns that I thought were Bird's-nest ferns. The fronds were so small that it was hard to tell what shape they were or would become. But I knew that I wanted them for their distinctive outline and to add points of interest—sort of like exclamation marks—to an indoor planting scheme.

Back home and nestled into new window boxes, they produced little pointy leaves protruding from an arrangement of potted plants. Soon it became apparent that they not only were growing faster than other new arrivals, but that they were growing into something I had not expected. The leaves took on deeper lobes. What had appeared in the babies as just a little green flat area across the surface of the pot began to spread out, turn brown, and develop layers covering the soil surface. It dawned on me that I didn't have Bird's-nests—I had stags!

Never having had a Staghorn fern, *Platycerium*, before, I began to do a little research to try to learn more about its background and its needs. Everything I read described the exact opposite of the conditions in which my ferns were, frankly, thriving!

My window boxes are indoors just under a sunny south-facing window. Stags like shade or filtered sunlight. My plants are still in pots, planted in soil. Stags are epiphytes, air plants, whose roots do not need, or even like, to be in the soil. They are grown on slabs of wood to make them think that they are clinging to the tree trunks of their native tropical

Staghorn Fern

forests. My plants survived very well during a period when our house temperature dipped alarmingly low while we were absent for a time during the winter. Stags like night temperatures of around fifty to sixty degrees. These direct contradictions only confirm what plant people already know—that nothing is certain and that we can be fooled most of the time.

But since I hope I am one of the people who can be fooled only some of the time, I will have to get with the program in order to keep these little ferns growing and healthy. When weather permits, I'll unpot them to help them remember that they are epiphytes. Any plant that is smart enough to produce two kinds of fronds to take care of its needs for nutrition and propagation is smart enough to remember where it came from.

First, let's take a look at those fronds. The large green fronds that resemble antlers, and that give the plant its common name, grow out in dramatic angles from the base of the plant. These are the fertile fronds that bear the spores that are the fern family's means of propagation. But stags grown as houseplants seldom produce spores and it probably is just as well, since the process of germinating them is complicated and best left to professionals. Alternatively, they can, and do, put out offsets that may be removed from the parent and grown to produce new stags. The brown fronds, called basal fronds, are sterile and grow into a round, flat disk that covers the plant's roots and provides its base of support. In effect, the plant makes its own pot!

Now isn't that clever? How do the genes know to separate the signals they send to the cells that are going to grow into either type of frond? Do they ever make a mistake and switch colors and functions? Sorry…just asking!

Fooling Around with Stags

When my little ones go outside for the summer, I will transplant or actually transfix them onto boards or slabs of wood or bark. The following directions are gleaned from a variety of houseplant guidebooks and gardening websites. Sorry—I cannot offer firsthand advice on this.

On the back of the board attach a hook or some kind of loop for a wire or chain to go through in order to hang it. Anticipate that the plant may become very heavy in the future if it does well, and use heavy-duty materials. Soak a good amount of long-fibered sphagnum moss in water for several hours. Prepare the mounting surface on the front of the board by tacking in some nails in a circumferential pattern somewhat larger than the fern. Place the soaked sphagnum moss in the center of this area, and lay the fern on it with the green fronds facing upward. Wrap the whole thing together with lightweight nylon fishing line, crossing from nail to opposite nail until the fern with its base of moss is securely mounted on the board.

Recommended conditions are bright light, but no direct sunlight, with moderate temperatures not dipping below fifty degrees at night. The biggest challenge is watering, and it can be messy. Soak the moss, and provide an area underneath the planting for the water to drip down into. Keep the moss moist, but not soggy, and allow it to almost dry between waterings. Another method is to plunge the whole thing into a large container of water at room temperature, and let it soak. Add a balanced fertilizer (20-20-20) to the water only once every quarter, and add fresh moss between the board and the basal fronds once a year. Respect its protective fuzzy surface.

Once they are out of the window box with all its wrong conditions, what will I do with my newly mounted stags? I might try suspending one on a chain over the bathtub where the humidity will be beneficial. The other might find a home under overhead lights with my other houseplants for company, going on occasional visits to the kitchen where the winter sunlight isn't too strong. Who knows? I might be surprised at how well they thrive in ideal conditions, but it won't be nearly as interesting!

I Love a Mystery

Q: It looks like the measles, but it's black.

It can be cleaned off, but it comes back.

It is persistent, nasty, and embarrassing.

What is it?

A: Sooty mold, but I didn't know that for a long time.

The history behind this little mystery is a long one. For many months, I had been battling the presence of a grimy layer of tiny black dots on my ivy plants. There were some strange things about it.

It didn't appear to do any damage to the plants, other than to make them look disagreeable. No leaves or leaf parts were eaten away or turning brown or curling up. The plants did look somewhat chlorotic, however, with leaves turning pale. This will be explained later.

The grime was inanimate. When I first scraped it off with a fingernail, I expected to see it move or wiggle. Other than staining my nail temporarily, nothing happened. So it was not a tiny insect at work.

Even more puzzling was that no other plants were affected. This led me to suspect that something specific to the ivy plant was attracting the grime.

It would come off, although it liked to cling a bit, with a shower bath under the kitchen spray hose. Over and over I wiped off the tiny black smudge by hand, only to watch it reappear. Finally, after a longer period of neglect and as part of my fall cleanup routine, I used a toothbrush dipped into a solution of half alcohol and half water, and scrubbed every leaf. Or at least I thought I had gotten every leaf.

Back it came a week later, and I then did what I should have done months before. Down I went to my local garden center with two leaves in a baggie, one with a little bit of shiny substance on the surface of the leaf, and the other with a good healthy dose of the black stuff on the leaf and its petiole. The good plant doctors there diagnosed the problem with the help of their encyclopedia of plant diseases. Sooty mold it was.

Sooty mold is a two-stage problem. It is defined as a fungus that develops on leaves and stems that have been hosts to insects such as aphids, whiteflies, and scales. One theory is that these insects secrete a sugary substance called honeydew as part of the feeding process, and this attracts the sooty mold. Another theory is that the plant itself secretes the honeydew, a sugary plant sap that then attracts the insects and the sooty mold. Sooty mold will appear wherever those sucking insects are active, which is another source of puzzlement to me. I have never seen any of these insects on my plants.

Could my ivy be secreting the little sugary sap without the stimulation of an insect? And why only the ivy?

Whitefly would be very obvious. All you have to do is move the plant, and clouds of the little rascals fly out. A large infestation of whitefly is almost impossible to get rid of. It's easier to destroy the plant and start over again. You'll know if you have whitefly.

Aphids ought to be equally obvious as they are visible although tiny. I rely on my resident ladybugs to take care of any aphids that may dare to show up, and, so far, that has worked well. I thought I would know if I have aphids, but maybe they are too tiny to see.

It may be scale insects, although if it is, they are microscopic.

The next move is to get rid of any possible insects, whatever they are. The first effort is to mix a solution of water and detergent, and douse the plant with it. Leave it on the plant for ten or fifteen minutes, and then wash it off with a strong spray from a garden or kitchen hose. Repeat every few days until it seems that the condition has disappeared. If that doesn't work, try an insecticide, spraying both under and around the leaves and covering the stems. Be sure to check the label before use as some plants cannot tolerate certain insecticides.

At the same time, inspect the other houseplants to see if there is any sign of either the pests themselves, or their honeydew, and treat them the same way.

Earlier I mentioned that one sign of damage to the plants was a slight case of chlorosis. You will know that you have chlorosis when leaves turn paler green than normal, or yellow, and often show signs of stunted growth, especially in the very young leaves. One cause of chlorosis is that sooty mold prevents the leaf from getting enough sunlight. A more common cause is that the plant is not receiving sufficient nutrients, which may be the result of an infestation. Noticing this, I had been feeding the plants iron to try to cure that problem. Once clear of the insects, and then the honeydew, and then the sooty mold, I'll try again to take care of the chlorosis!

Be on the lookout for sooty mold on outdoor plants as well. Azaleas, laurels, myrtles, and many other ornamentals that are favorite foods for sucking insects will end up with honeydew. Plants under trees visited by aphids and other sucking insects can also be infected.

So the mystery is partially solved. I've learned about sooty mold and what causes it. But some questions remain. Why only the ivy? What is the microscopic pest it harbors, if it harbors one at all? Maybe people who grow plants never do have all the answers, and maybe that's part of the challenge and the charm.

Taming the Wild Bromeliads

This large family of plants, the Bromeliaceae, has strange but wonderful relatives that would hardly recognize each other. Some are terrestrial, growing like normal plants in the ground. Others are saxicolous, growing on what seem to be rock faces and stone cliffs. Some are epiphytic, or air plants, wildly swinging and swaying from the limbs of trees and shrubs.

Most of the epiphytic bromeliads originate in the tropical forests of Central and South America where they grow all over the place, literally. They hang from the tree limbs in the high canopy. They lodge in little niches in tree trunks. They seem to spring out of nowhere, their foliage creating fascinating shapes and forms. They compete with each other for space on tree branches, lianas, and vines, shoving each other out of the way and creating dense miniforests of their own.

It would be difficult to maintain these epiphytes as houseplants unless one has an enormous amount of hanging space indoors or a home greenhouse. Fortunately, there are many species of terrestrial bromeliads that can be tamed to be totally content in pots, and are among the easiest of houseplants to care for.

In the tropical forests, bromeliad roots anchor the plant down in the winds and rains of their environment. Most of the roots form a small tight web that enables them both to support the plant without pieces breaking off and also to dig into the material to which they are attached. They can absorb some moisture from the tropical rainstorms, but it quickly drains off, running down the tree trunks or dripping off the branches.

This gives us a clue as to how they want to be potted—in a porous, fibrous mix that duplicates as closely as possible the bits and pieces they locate in the wild. Orchid potting mixes work well. Use a small pot—the roots like to huddle close together.

In their wisdom, and in the wonderful world of nature's survivors, these plants have developed a unique structure to obtain the water they need. Most of the more popular bromeliads we cultivate have leaves in the shape of an urn, or vase, at their base. This rosette-like form catches and holds water that is then absorbed by the plant as needed.

This gives us a clue as to how it wants to be watered. Just "fill 'er up!" If your house temperature is warm enough (about sixty degrees or more during the day) that water should evaporate while it nourishes the plant and should not become stagnant. If the water is not totally absorbed in a few days, empty out the little "cup" and start over again. Maintain the high humidity level preferred by these plants by keeping the pots on a tray filled with pebbles or peastone kept constantly moist.

In the wild, the plant's cup-like structure catches more than rainwater. Insects, vegetative debris from leaves and twigs, and sometimes little tree frogs fall into the cup and cannot get out. The plant, however, is not carnivorous, as are the pitcher plant and other tropical plants with similar structural parts. It does not actually eat or absorb the insects and frogs themselves. But in the decaying process, nutrients are released into the water and absorbed by the plant. The cups of bromeliads in the wild are a miniature maze of drowned fauna and decaying flora. We would not want to pick one to take home!

This gives us a clue as to how it should be fed, adding fertilizer to both the cup and the roots. Most houseplant guides recommend a light feeding: one-quarter strength balanced fertilizer (20-20-20) once every month or two. Your bromeliad will think that it is hosting a *coqui*, the tiny, noisy tree frogs of Puerto Rico! Since most of the plants grow under the canopy, and some are quite far down near the forest floor, they thrive in fairly low light levels and certainly do not need bright sunlight.

Blooming can be problematic. Occurring only on mature plants, you may have to wait several years for a blossom. The flower will last a long time, however. When it fades, the parent plant will begin to die, putting out pups or offsets in the process. It may be a total mess as the leaves die. When that happens, knock the plant out of its pot, gently dislodge the pups, and pot them up on their own in a medium as described above. Then start the long wait again!

Bromeliad

If a mature plant is hesitant to bloom, it can often be helped along using a trick reported by Thalassa Cruso in her classic how-to, *Making Things Grow*, New York, NY, Alfred A. Knopf, Inc., 1969. Cut an apple into pieces, place one or two of them around the plant depending on the plant's size, and enclose the whole thing in a large plastic bag tied tightly. Place it away from sunlight, and ignore it for a month. You may have a flower spike when you open it up. The theory is that the gas released by the rotting apple may stimulate bud formation, much as the gas released by rotting debris in nature helps the bromeliad to initiate bloom.

Most of the bromeliads are interesting and colorful enough without bloom. The *Aechmea fasciata,* Urn plant or Silver Vase, has beautiful thick blue-green leaves curving upward in its vase-like form, sometimes mottled with darker stripes and covered with a fine powder-like silver sheen. When, and if, it blooms, the blossom is a dramatic pink, single spike rising out of the cup. Other bromeliads include the tillandsias, neoregalias, vriesias, and earth stars, all with colorful foliage.

Whether anchored in a pot, or hanging from the branches of a tree, your tamed bromeliads will love to spend the summer outdoors. And, if they've never bloomed for you, trick them with an apple next winter!

Crown of Thorns—
A Dangerous Beauty

B efore you read about the legends connected with *Euphorbia milii*, you really must have a mental image of it. The stems sport some of the wickedest long spines on any plant I know of. The leaves are small and the tiny red flowers, actually the bracts of the plant, are colored and shaped like little drops of blood. It is a striking plant and all the more so when called by its common name, Crown of Thorns.

This plant can be a vivid focus for meditation during the Lenten season while maintaining its reputation as a hardy and durable houseplant. Legends about the real Crown of Thorns abound. For example, it was preserved by the followers of Christ and passed reverently from one place to another, while its leaves remained green. Another legend describes how the flowers of the species, originally white, turned red after having been stained by the blood of Christ. Other stories follow the routes of individual spines of the crown as they were carefully preserved and carried as relics to the earliest Christian communities.

Wikipedia, the online encyclopedia, has a good article on this subject, but it suggests two different plants as sources for the Crown of Thorns. One is the species we're discussing, *E. milii*, native to Madagascar, which had been brought to the Middle East before the time of Christ and therefore would have been available. Another theory holds that the thorns used to plait the crown came from the jujube tree, found in abundance at that time around Jerusalem.

Some of the euphorbias are succulents, having evolved to exist in dry desert conditions. Their thorns, of course, serve to protect the plants and their supply of water from predators, although not all members of the family have this coat of armor. The plant we're discussing is a terrific houseplant, and it is surprising that it is not as widely used as it could be. If the spines aren't a problem for youngsters in your household, if you have good, heavy gloves for handling it, and if you give it the right conditions, this plant can give you years of enjoyment.

My plant is a dwarf, about twelve inches tall, which makes it manageable in a collection of houseplants. It blooms all year for me in its south-facing indoor window box where it receives full sun and warm conditions. Water it generously and then allow the soil to almost dry out before watering again, but do not let the roots dry out. Succulents like to have a lot of water once in a while, just as they do in nature, but guard against over-watering, which can cause pale leaves and root rot. Give it a light feeding two or three times from spring until fall, using a high potash fertilizer (the third number on the label).

From time to time the leaves may fall off, especially if the temperature falls below fifty-five degrees, but they will grow back in warmer temperatures. What we call the flowers are actually tiny bracts that surround the minuscule yellow flowers. They are smaller versions of their cousin poinsettias, whose little yellow flowers are negligible by comparison to the showy red bracts. Flowering is most intense during the warm summer months.

Crown of Thorns

Propagating this thorny creature is tricky, but it can be done wearing heavy gloves. Cut off a side branch where it meets the main stem, or the tip of a branch just below a leaf, making a sharp cut with a razor blade. Take several cuttings at a time to help ensure that at least one will be successful! Strip any leaves away from the ends of the new cuttings and beware of latex oozing from the cut areas. Take care—this is poisonous and may cause blisters on your skin or damage to your eyes. Keep any youngsters away from the procedure, and wash your hands and tools well afterward.

Spray the parent plant and its cut area with water, and dip the new little cuttings into some water to staunch the flow of latex. Set the cuttings aside (again, out of reach of little hands) for a few days to allow calluses to form over the cut portions. When the callus is evident, dip the end of each cutting into a fresh hormone rooting powder, like Rootone, and plant it in a cactus/succulent potting mix or a standard potting mix to which you have added about one-third perlite or coarse sand (not beach sand).

Most of the signs of distress in the Crown of Thorns, such as shriveling leaves, blackening, and soft stem ends, are caused by too much humidity and overwatering. A good air flow around the plant is helpful, both to maintain good circulation and also to help prevent little insects from settling on the leaves. In the winter, if you are comfortable with your indoor temperature, chances are that your Crown of Thorns will be comfortable, too.

If you see a reference to *Euphorbia splendens*, it is the same plant now enjoying a new name, *milii*. Mr. Milius was a baron, once governor of the island of Bourbon, who began to cultivate this plant in France in the 1800s. Dr. Euphorbus was a Greek physician who lived during the time of Christ and was the personal physician to the King of Numidia, which is present-day Algeria. Perhaps the king was a plant hunter who brought the plant from Madagascar to the Middle East? Upon discovering this plant, however he did it, he named it after his physician. Who knows why? I'll bet that Dr. Euphorbus cured the king after some latex dropped on him!

Stones Get a Life

R emember pet rocks? That fad from the '70s?
People actually spent money for a rock that was the lowest maintenance possible pet. It didn't eat or drink anything, it did not need to be taken out although it loved to ride around in your pocket, and it didn't bark at night. It never complained when left alone and was always there when you needed it.

If you loved pet rocks, you will love Living Stones. These are plants that are almost as trouble-free as pet rocks and are the best rock imitators in the plant world. They blend into their stony habitat so skillfully that one is hard-pressed to spot them in the wild. And when they bloom, it's like a sci-fi experience. Talk about weird!

The botanical name *Lithops* comes from the Greek *lithos* (stone) and *opsis* (face), and the plants are commonly called Living Stones because that is exactly what they look like. In the plant world, these little critters may have the highest IQ and the best ability to predict danger and defend themselves. When it comes to survival of the fittest, lithops win hands down.

Members of the succulent family Mesembryanthemaceae, thankfully called Mesembs for short, they are found in arid, desolate areas of South Africa and Namibia where they have had to go to great lengths to survive. They have done this by reducing themselves to a very small size that is totally devoted to water storage. Two succulent leaves, smooth and low

Lithops

to the ground, are all that can be seen, and even they can shrink down almost below the pebbly surface if extreme conditions warrant evasive action. Masters of camouflage, these leaves have developed markings and colors that closely resemble the patterns and colors in the stones surrounding them, thereby contributing different characteristics to varieties within the plant family. Even grazing animals, desperate for water during periods of drought, will easily pass them by.

There is a little fissure between the two leaves containing the meristem, the growth cells of the plant. Here the taproot grows downward to seek out whatever water it can. From the same meristem, and when a lithops is about three years old, reproduction will begin. Following the seasonal rains, the fissure will separate and a bud will grow upward to produce a flower and a new pair of leaves. Watching the flowers emerge from the "stones" is truly one of the most amazing sights in nature! When the new leaves mature and grow fleshy, drawing their water and nutrients from the older leaves, the latter shrivel away and die off.

From this description, it is easy to see that lithops can be ideal pet rocks in your houseplant collection. Their needs are simple but important to understand. They have been smart enough to stay alive under certain conditions that must be provided in order to have them think that they are back in their native land.

Light and water are the key ingredients to success with almost all houseplants, but especially lithops. They require four to five hours of direct sunlight per day; morning sun is best. If grown in a south-facing window, they should be shaded or given filtered light during the afternoon. In the spring, after a winter of less intense light, they should be reintroduced to direct sunlight gradually in order to prevent sunburn. Think of them as people, and be sensible about a sudden shock.

Watering lithops is one time when we should not think of them as people, at least not normal people who need water. Basically, they are watered during spring and fall. They go dormant during the summer months and should be given only enough water to prevent them from shriveling. In the fall, after the dormancy period, lithops begin their flowering cycle and should be watered deeply in order to get the growth going. Water enough to get it down to the taproot, just as Mother Nature would do with her seasonal rains. Allow the soil to dry out almost completely between waterings. If the soil stays damp around the plant, it is likely to cause rot.

After the fall growth cycle, withhold water altogether to allow the new leaves to draw their water naturally from the old leaves and to allow the old leaves to shrivel away. Mist occasionally during this period. Once spring approaches, you can gradually begin to water again. With the onset of summer and the plant's period of dormancy, gradually withhold water and you are back to the beginning of the cycle.

Lithops are easily cultivated from seed that can be extracted from the seed capsule. The seeds are available also from several Internet sources. Sprinkle the tiny seeds directly into a well-drained sandy medium, perhaps sand mixed with a fine gravel. Leave it uncovered, and mist just enough to prevent the seeds from drying out. When the seedlings are large enough, transplant them into their permanent pots. Provide extra drainage capability by adding one part sand (not beach sand) to two parts of your soil mix, and plant them in pots deep enough to accommodate their taproots. Set a few pebbles or stones on the surface of the soil for company and to give the Living Stones something to imitate, and sprinkle a light layer of sand or thin gravel over the surface. Obviously, they will lend themselves very well to dish gardens accompanied by stones and other succulents.

Just like pet rocks, these little creatures are irresistible. They are so cute, and funny, that they will win your heart. Run your fingers over their smooth surfaces once in a while to let them know that you know that they're alive. They love to be petted!

Put Your Jade Plant in Your Will

There is something about the jade plant that is endearing. It is somewhat comical with branches that defy overall form and shape, a thick trunk that is out of scale with its small leaves, and an awkward look. In spite of, or maybe because of, this, *Crassula argentea* has a way of commanding attention and affection. I ought to know. I am currently making a third attempt at growing a pair of jades to maturity.

Maturity for a jade seems to never come. People report inheriting a jade from their parents and then handing it down to the next generation! Growing slowly, it can reach a large size, three feet or more, if its caretaker does the right thing. I didn't, so I am starting over.

Two giants that I had cherished for close to twenty years reached sizes of around three feet before they succumbed to a major infestation of scales. In spite of months of swabbing with alcohol and scraping with my fingernails, the scales persisted and finally, in tears, I had to destroy the plants. Most recently, two babies that were intended to replace them froze when I left them outside too long in the fall. Challenging history, I now am about two years into another pair.

Jades in their early years are small specimens to be used in dish gardens and small arrangements. They are among the most adaptable of houseplants. They do best in full sun for at least three or four hours a day and will develop strong trunks and a little reddish tinge or edge to their leaves if given this amount of sunlight. When the plants mature and if they grow in sunlight, they will produce quantities of tiny white or pinkish flowers. But they will also do fine in strong indirect light, or behind a sheer curtain that filters the sunlight.

They can swing with temperature variations, preferring a daytime reading of between sixty-five and seventy with a nighttime drop into the fifties, but will be OK with nineties during the day and forties at night but no lower. This is a clue that they are succulents, members of one of those plant families that originated in the various dry and arid regions of the globe. As survivors of such harsh conditions, succulents adapted themselves to temperature and water variations. Through millions of years of evolution, the stems and leaves of these plants became fleshy reservoirs that filled up during the rainy season and then provided water as needed during long droughts.

Thus, jades like a lot of water once in a while but not on a regular basis, and they like to dry out somewhat between waterings. In winter they require even less water, only enough to prevent the fleshy leaves from wrinkling. Feed them very seldom with a diluted balanced fertilizer (20-20-20). They need good drainage and actually thrive in a terra cotta pot rather than in plastic.

When young and in a faster growth mode, the jade may outgrow its pot. Repot in the spring using a potting mix of one part loam, one part peat moss or leaf mold, and one part builders sand (not beach sand) or grit. Add a bit of superphosphate, ground limestone, and a little 5-10-5 fertilizer. Place the plant outdoors in a semishady location to prevent the strong sun from scorching the leaves. Later on, it can get full sunlight for a few hours a day. It will require more frequent waterings at this time of the year.

Now, other than getting big-time scales, scorching the leaves with summer sun, or freezing the plant at under forty degrees, what can go wrong?

Incorrect watering habits can have serious consequences. If the leaves turn black and fall off, it is a signal that the stems and roots have rot and that the plant is too cold and too wet. Allow it to dry out for a month or more, and keep the nighttime temperature in the fifties. Cut away the blackened area, dust with a fungicide, continue to dry it out, and then repot.

Jade.

If the leaves dry up and drop off, it's another problem. In summer, it may be too dry or may have been overwatered. Check the moisture level in the soil and adjust accordingly. If it begins to grow long spindly stems with small sparse leaves, this is a signal that the plant is straining to get more light. Move it into a sunnier position.

Scales are not the only pests attracted to this plant. Mealybugs love jades and will lodge in the little crevices where the leaves meet the stems. At the first sight of these white, woolly patches, remove them with a cotton swab dipped in alcohol, and then spray the plant with an insecticide (not Malathion—it has a disastrous effect on jade plant leaves). If the plant is not growing, or looks sickly, check the roots for mealybugs. If they have penetrated to the roots, wash the soil off the roots and douse the root ball in an insecticide solution (again, not Malathion). Allow it to dry, and then repot it in fresh potting medium and a clean pot. Do not water for several weeks.

Start your jade plant now, and put it in your will. Your grandchildren will love it!

5

The Shopper in You

Norfolk Island Pine

Bulbs—Living Gifts with Love

A living gift is a beautiful gift. Blooming and foliage plants look oh-so-wonderful in their four-color photos, in catalogs, and on websites. And it is oh-so-easy to order them, have them wrapped and sent, and to have the gift cards written as if you wrote them yourself.

The trouble is that you didn't write them yourself. In fact, you didn't do anything yourself except make the phone call or click and pull out your credit card. Turn the living gift into a loving gift by doing it yourself.

If your hobby is horticulture, and you love to propagate, you must have several offspring from your collection ready to go, potted up in attractive clean pots and healthy as only young plants can be, untouched by human neglect! If so, congratulations! But right now most of us are saying "I coulda, and I shoulda!" We didn't plan far enough ahead of the approaching holiday season, we have a few spider plantlets not yet rooted, divisions of clivia are not yet robust enough to give away, and our ivy transplanted from summer containers is looking a bit feeble. What to do?

The answer is bulbs. Most of the traditional bulbs, like hyacinths and tulips, require a cold dormant period of about three months in order to bloom. If it is too late in the season to acquire good quality bulbs, make a note for next year to start earlier. Once the bulbs come on the market around the end of September, pot up your choice in attractive pots, include a little note to the recipient, and perhaps include a photo and directions for care. And take credit for planning ahead and being thoughtful.

But it usually is not too late for amaryllis or *Tazetta*, a.k.a. paper-whites.

What we call amaryllis is really *Hippeastrum.* The true *Amaryllis* genus is the belladonna lily, not a houseplant. But common usage has tagged this gorgeous bulb with the name, so that is what we call it. Amaryllis has almost taken over the market in holiday plants. They get bigger and more colorful and are foolproof, dramatic, and drop-dead gorgeous.

Popular nurseries and garden supply houses feature amaryllis bulbs in their holiday catalogs. They arrive potted up in pots or wicker baskets or can be ordered as bare bulbs. They are not cheap, and they do not arrive in bloom. Ready to go, yes, but your recipient still must wait for the full performance in about eight weeks.

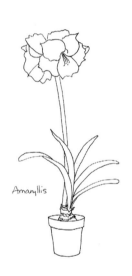

Amaryllis

A less expensive route is to buy one of the kits widely found in the market in the late fall, containing everything you will need. Bulb, soil, pot, directions, and less than three minutes of your time will result in a large stalk and flower, probably within two months of potting it up. But purists will shop for bare bulbs that they can handle and press, to be sure that their quality is the best. When buying bulbs, it is important to remember that they already contain the flower within, ready to burst into bloom when watered and fed. It stands to reason, therefore, that the larger the bulb the larger the flower—and the better formed and shaped the bulb, ditto the flower. The same reasoning applies to the soil used to pot them up.

If you can enrich the growing medium with a light feeding, your bulb will get off to a much better start and will do better in its renewal period for the next bloom.

Follow the directions for potting, being careful to leave about half of the bulb above the soil line. If you are starting from scratch, add a little crockery to a clean pot, fill it about half full with your potting medium, adding a bit of ground limestone, and then snuggle the bulb into the soil basal plate down adding more soil up to about one-half the size of the bulb. Give it a good watering, and keep it in a warm location in good light but not direct sunlight, at least not yet. Do not water it again until the first tiny green shoot appears at the top of the bulb. When this occurs, begin to keep the soil moist and feed it about twice a month with a half-strength balanced fertilizer (20-20-20). Once the shoot starts its upward surge, and some leaves appear, you can move it into sunlight to hasten its bloom. Be sure to rotate it so that the stem will grow straight upward and not turn into a "leaning tower!"

The *Tazetta* are the easiest bulbs to pot up, because you don't even need to pot them. They are happy just resting on pebbles or white marble chips set into an attractive container. They are inexpensive, beautiful, and fragrant. Commonly called paperwhites for their color and texture, they are sold in garden centers and in some gift shops. Again, selecting your own plump, firm bulbs that are well formed, with no bulges or scars, will ensure more perfect flowers. While shopping for the bulbs, keep your eyes open for interesting containers. This is a big part of your gift.

Using marble chips, the planting process is easy. Fill the bowl or container about three-quarters full, and set the bulbs gently on them as close together as possible. The more bulbs you set together, using an odd number, the better the show will be. I think that five are the minimum, and eleven or thirteen are fantastic! It is fun to pot one up in a little mug, or teacup, for a child. Fill with water, just up to the basal plates from which the roots will grow, and then add another thin layer of pebbles. This is one time when you don't have to worry about drainage in the pot.

Move the paperwhites gradually into brighter light as the roots develop, and keep the water level constant at the basal plates of the bulbs. A gentle tug at the bulb will tell you when it is well rooted. Provide cool nights, and keep the bulbs out of direct sunlight to help lengthen their bloom. And, since they cannot be recycled, just throw them out in the compost pile after they fade.

It's fun to give paperwhites before they bloom, especially to children. One morning, I answered the telephone to hear an excited little voice exclaim, "Nana, they're popping!"

Why Bother with a Gloxinia?

There is an old saying that, "a want ain't necessarily a need." I try to remember this as I visit favorite garden shops and resist the seductive displays in garden catalogs.

Just like people, houseplants have wants that can't always be satisfied and may not necessarily be needs. Some plants can get by on just their "wants" and be reasonably happy under lots of different conditions. But not all!

For the Florist Gloxinia, *Sinningia speciosa*, a want *is* necessarily a need, and it must be provided. This is one of the fussiest of houseplants, even for professional growers. It must have the right conditions or else.

This gloxinia, one member of the large family of gesneriads, is not a true gloxinia, although they are related. It's too boring to try to recount how and why the name got changed, and only a professional taxonomist would care, but Herr Gloxin of Strasburg, Germany, would be pleased to know that his name has prevailed in describing this especially beautiful member of the species.

Our gloxinia is descended from an accident, a "chance" seedling discovered by a Scottish gardener as a result of hybridizing two Brazilian species. The gardener, John Fyfe, was taken with the unexpected beauty and charm of his offspring, different from any of its immediate ancestors. This plant held its head of symmetrical flowers high instead of drooping or nodding. Mr. Fyfe knew a good thing when he saw it and proceeded to propagate it for posterity. Today's gloxinias all are the descendants of that one lucky accident.

Many gesneriads have tubular or bell-shaped flowers to accommodate their principal pollinator, the hummingbird. The gloxinias we purchase as houseplants tend to be large with flowers measuring up to three inches in diameter and large oval-shaped velvety leaves fanning out under the flowers. The color range for the flowers and their variegation seems to increase every year as breeders come up with new tones and hues of white, red, pink, lavender, and purple, some with white borders, some with whitish or darkish centers, plain or ruffled, single or double—take your pick.

This beauty comes with a price, however. It is a demanding plant to care for, and it is quite difficult to propagate. If you have kept a gloxinia going through the winter, congratulations! You must have done everything right. It wants and needs bright, indirect light in order to flower. It wants and needs space, both for its roots and for its top growth. It needs to be warm, meaning nighttime temperatures of sixty-five degrees or warmer and daytime temperatures of around seventy-five degrees. It does not like to sit in a draft, or even be caught in a chilly breeze!

Watering must be done carefully with tepid water and just a little bit at a time in order to keep the soil moist but not too wet. Like its cousin, the African violet, it does not want its leaves to get wet—not even a drop, and the new buds also must be kept dry. Bottom watering works well, but do not let the pot sit in water past the time when the soil is moist.

The gloxinia likes a little food with its water, which can be provided by adding a bit of balanced fertilizer (20-20-20) to the water once a week. Provide extra humidity by keeping the pot on a tray of moist pebbles. This will help keep the leaves from breaking, which they are prone to do.

By this time, you must be thinking "why bother?" But that isn't all. The true test of your devotion comes with aftercare when you give the plant a period of dormancy. When the flowers have faded, begin to water less frequently, and then stop altogether and allow the leaves to die off. Keep the tuberous stem totally dry and ignore the plant for two to four months. At that point, it will wake up and begin to send out some new green growth. When that happens, repot the tuber in fresh potting medium, preferably an African violet potting mix. The tuber should be placed with the hollow section on the top and close to the soil surface. Water it well, continue to water and feed it as before, and set it in bright indirect light. Flowers should reappear in another four months.

Gloxinia

Propagating a gloxinia is challenging, even for the professionals. Leaf cuttings, leaf layering, or growing from seed are the best means. Leaf layering is done in the same manner as might be done with the large leaves of Rex begonias. The best leaf candidates are the vigorous middle-aged leaves on the plant, not the oldest and not the youngest.

Cut off the leaf, and place it flat on top of a moist potting mix or builders sand (not beach sand). With a sharp razor blade, cut across the veins of the leaf, and be sure that the cut edges are in contact with the mix or sand and will stay that way. You might brush a little fresh Rootone, the hormone rooting powder, into the cut. Cover with clear plastic wrap or glass, and place it in a bright location, but not in sunlight. Keep the mixture or sand moist, but not soggy wet. Watch the cut places to see when the first new little plantlets begin to form, and then remove the covering bit by bit. Pot up the new little plants, and provide the care they need as described above.

The answer to "why bother?" Well, when a healthy, well-grown gloxinia is in full flower, that answer will be obvious. You will want, and need, to bother!

Flu and Fungus Season

S tanding in line for my flu shot, I had plenty of time to reflect on the seasonal hazards we face, flu among them. And, since we think of our plants as people, I began to think about their seasonal hazards. And there are plenty.

Plants get sick, just like us. Sometimes they can be cured, with our help, and sometimes they can't. But we can only help them if we know what's wrong, and this is where most of us who are amateur growers fall down. Very few people really enjoy studying up on pests and diseases, a yucky subject. But if we're going to keep plants indoors, we need a hospital wing.

Plants were not created to live indoors. It follows that those that have gained status as favorite houseplants are those best able to adapt to this foreign indoor environment. Just as with people, the first line of defense should be prevention. Begin with your purchase—buy only healthy plants. Don't fall for a bargain-priced plant that looks as if it's in trouble.

Once at home, much can be done to keep plants in healthy condition, free of insect pests and diseases, but it requires constant vigilance. To the three basics of plant care, light, water, and food, add ventilation and cleanliness. How we provide these basics has a lot to do with a healthy plant environment and imitating Mother Nature as closely as possible. This is especially true when it comes to watering.

It's generally agreed that most plant problems are caused by watering, either too much or too little. A yellowing leaf, for example, can be the result of either, and only the caregiver knows the answer. In nature, when the heavens open up and we get a downpour, plants are ecstatic. They get a good drink, their foliage gets laundered, and their nutrients have fresh carriers into their root systems. Not so inside. Wet foliage and stems are the most common cause of fungal diseases on houseplants.

Let's take leaf spot as an example of a fungus that plagues many of us in the winter. Picture a fairly large leaf of a dracaena, a clivia, or a schefflera, looking pretty good except for a large brownish patch surrounded wholly or partially by a yellowish ring, perhaps with little bumps within it. The brown area is thin and dry and somewhat papery in texture. The brown spot is random, not following the veining pattern of the leaf. Chances are that this is not the only spot on the plant, but if it is, we might be in luck.

The first thing to do is to cut off that leaf, and get rid of it. The next thing to do is to knock the plant out of its pot, and look at the roots. If the root ball is still firm and the roots are whitish and compact, then the plant is not yet badly infected. In this case, trim away any limp roots, replace the plant in its pot, and withhold water until the plant literally wilts and bends over. Then begin to water very gradually, being careful not to get any of the foliage or stems wet. If the root ball is mushy and the roots are limp and dark, we can try to save the plant by root-pruning it back to where the roots seem healthy, taking out enough foliage to somewhat match the smaller size of the root ball, and then repot it in a smaller pot, again withholding water until the plant truly looks wilted. Then begin to water very gradually.

Of course, you can always just throw it out and start over again!

Fungus loves dark, damp, and cool conditions. No matter how strong indoor light is, it is less than the plant would receive outside. That lower light, combined with water left on the leaves and cool nights is a gilt-edged invitation for a fungus to move in. This can be prevented by keeping the foliage dry, watering carefully into the soil only, or bottom watering by allowing the pot to sit in a pan of water until the soil surface is moist. Then drain excess water out of the pot. Do not let the pot sit in a saucer of water, again as a guard against root rot. Water in the morning so that the foliage will be dry going into the cooler night temperature. A fungus cannot reproduce in dry conditions.

To these watering guidelines, add plenty of light, a small fan to provide air circulation, and sparse feedings, especially during winter months when the plants are not in high-growth mode.

A recommended nonorganic spray for treating plants with fungus is to combine one teaspoon of baking soda, half a teaspoon of liquid hand soap, and half a teaspoon of vegetable oil in one quart of warm water. Spray early in the day every two weeks. Repeat three times. Eliminate the baking soda for other plant diseases and to help control insect pests.

Just a warning word about plant bacteria. A bacterial leaf spot can look a lot like a fungus, but it will not have that yellow halo, and it is wet. An infected leaf will look as if it has melted, be mushy, and will often smell bad. The roots will smell bad also. The leaf spot often will follow the veining pattern of the leaf, at least more so than a fungus will. Treat it as you would a fungus.

So, let's hope that there will be no fungus among us this season. There, I've finally said it!

Lily White Symbol for Easter

The Easter lily takes its common name from the most significant holy day in the Christian calendar, and it does so as a symbol in a long tradition. Symbols exist as suggestions and reminders of virtue and vice, life and death, and so forth. And lilies have always symbolized the good, the pure, and the holy.

The unblemished whiteness of its petals—lily white—no doubt gave rise to its association with purity and innocence—lily pure. The lily has always been associated with womankind rather than mankind. In an ancient tradition, Eve, no longer a symbol of innocence as she left the Garden of Eden, wept in remorse, and where those tears fell to the earth lilies grew, thereby establishing themselves as symbols of the virtue of repentance. This is a nice thought, although it might be argued that Eve's tears were caused by more than remorse.

Moving right along, an ancient fable tells us that the first lilies were nourished with the milk of Hera, the Greek goddess of love and marriage. Another giant step in time brings us to the Virgin Mary. The lily, representing purity and holiness, has been associated with her in numerous legends, paintings, and religious ceremonies right down to the present day.

And whoever coined the term "gilding the lily?"

My Easter lily has its own interesting history. *Lilium longiflorum* is native to the Ryukyu Islands of Japan, where it flourished as a bulb product until the start of World War II. Up until that point, the Japanese were dominating the production and export of Easter lilies to the United States. In 1919, a World War I soldier, Louis Houghton, had brought a load of bulbs to the south coast of Oregon as gifts to his neighbors and friends. They and their descendants had continued to cultivate them on a small scale. But after Pearl Harbor, the Japanese source of lily bulbs was cut off and their value skyrocketed. Those hobbyists in Oregon and California who were still growing the offspring of Houghton's lilies discovered that they had a cash cow on their hands, and the business spread. By the end of World War II, there were well over a thousand growers producing bulbs all along the northern Pacific coast.

Requirements for growing the lilies, especially in large numbers, proved to be somewhat demanding, and inevitably the number of producers dwindled and the geographical area shrank. Today, the "Easter Lily Capital of the World" comprises ten farms in a small, foggy, coastal marine region sharing the Oregon–California state line. Here, in Del Norte County, California, and Curry County, Oregon, over 95 percent of all the bulbs for the world's Easter commercial market are produced. We're talking millions of bulbs! The mild climate in this protected bay area, the rich soils, abundant rainfall, and the reliability of this climate over the years have combined to offer ideal conditions for the industry.

Easter Lily

Growing lilies is a multiyear task. The bulbs start out as offsets separated from their mother bulbs when the mothers are harvested. After several cycles of replanting, digging up, and replanting again, the bulbs are large and mature enough for the market. They are shipped to greenhouse growers all over North America, and these growers face a challenge in forcing unlike that faced when forcing other plants.

It's difficult enough to force a plant

into flower for a specific date, such as a flower show or Mother's Day. It's another to conform to the moveable date that is Easter. As a kid, I learned that Easter falls on "the first Sunday after the first full moon after the twenty-first of March," which means that it can occur anytime between March 21 and April 25. The growers must force the plants into flower to hit their peak bloom just before Easter Sunday. They admit that their crop has the narrowest holiday sales window, typically about two weeks, as compared to the poinsettia's four to six weeks between Thanksgiving and Christmas.

Now that we know all this about the Easter lily, we're going to appreciate it even more and want to purchase one of the best. Select a plant that has several partly opened or unopened buds to ensure a longer blooming period. Look for foliage that is dark green all the way down to the soil line, an indication of a healthy root system. If the leaves appear wilted, the roots could be rotten. You will see Easter lilies being marketed in paper or plastic sleeves. Avoid them if possible, as the plants deteriorate if kept sleeved too long.

Your lily will do fine in bright indirect light and in the moderately cool temperature of your home. Keep the soil moist and well drained. Some people like to remove the yellow anthers before the pollen begins to spread itself around in order to keep the petals lily white. In warm-temperate areas of the country, the lilies can be planted outdoors to produce blooms for another season.

Enjoy your Easter lily ... unless you have a cat! For some reason, members of the lily family are highly toxic to cats, and consumption can be fatal if untreated. If you share your home with a cat, you might prefer to celebrate this holiday with an Easter cactus.

What Do I Do Now?

It used to be easy, back before globalization, air freight, and the houseplant boom. Back when the mandatory Christmas plant was a poinsettia and when they only came in red. And it was easiest with poinsettias. We just lived with them until the season changed, and then we threw them out.

I still do. Throw out the poinsettias, that is. Partly because I consider them to be among the ugliest plants in creation and partly because it is almost impossible to bring the original back into full color for next Christmas, even if I wanted to. I don't, but see below if you want to.

Now it's hard. Garden centers and florists promote lots of choices for holiday giving. We receive many different, sometimes unfamiliar, plants as gifts—and then what? We still have the choice to throw them out, remembering who is boss. Or, we can think of the winter months as a time to learn about basic plant care, to fine-tune knowledge and, eventually, to propagate if that is what we want to do.

As always, begin by thinking of your gift plant as a person, but this time as a person who has been under a lot of stress. It's like taking someone out of a storm into your home. If the plant is in bloom, it has most likely been forced into it, and that takes a lot out of a plant. Some never recover. Others will be OK given the right conditions and a little TLC.

Blooming plants come from controlled greenhouse conditions where the temperatures are kept cool, both for the plants and for reasons of economy. Replicating the cool daytime temperatures, in the sixty to seventy degree range, bright light with a few hours of weak winter sunlight, and just enough water to keep the soil moist will provide good care for the Christmas cacti, azaleas, kalanchoe, anthurium, and Rieger begonias. As they probably have been overfed in the forcing process, put them on a sparse diet of little to no fertilizer for a few months. When we get into the spring months, their needs will vary and can be adjusted accordingly. Exceptions to the basic care outlined above are the poinsettia, cyclamen, a jasmine to some degree, a Norfolk Island pine, the Jerusalem cherry, ornamental pepper plants, and the many orchids.

Poinsettias (*Euphorbia pulcherrima*) like sun or bright light during the day and cooler temperatures at night and just enough water to stay moist. When the bracts fade or drop off in spring or early summer, take stem cuttings from the plant, root them in sand or a sterile medium, and pot them up. Set the rooted cuttings outdoors in light shade or filtered sunlight for the summer where they will grow healthy, but all green, foliage. Once fall arrives, it's time to give the poinsettia at least fourteen hours of darkness every night. If it receives even the least little bit of light at night during this period, the bracts will not turn red, pink, or white, and

Norfolk Island Pine

you will have a green poinsettia for Christmas! Keep it in a room where the lights never go on in the evening or in a closet (bringing it out during the day) or put a cloth over its head in the evening, birdcage style. Whatever works! Continue to water lightly, but don't feed it.

Cyclamen (*C. persicum*) is the perfect gift choice for friends who like to keep their houses cold. (Refer to "Cyclamen—Touching Elegance" in this book.) If you have an unheated spare bedroom, or a breezeway, pop your cyclamen there whenever you don't need to show it off, and it will be happy. Just don't forget about it! A cyclamen likes to be well-watered but also well drained, and it likes bright light but not direct sunlight. Feed it lightly occasionally, and it should continue to bloom well for several months.

Jasmine (*Jasminum polyanthum*) is taking its well-deserved place as a holiday gift plant in garden centers and catalogs. It likes to be kept cool, below sixty-five degrees, and loves humidity that can be provided by keeping it on a tray of moist pebbles or peastone. If your jasmine is in a hanging basket, which many are, hang it near a source of humidity. Keep the soil moderately moist, but do not feed it.

A Norfolk Island pine (*Araucaria heterophylla*), often used as a mini Christmas tree, wants as much direct light as possible, which means winter sunlight. Turn it ninety degrees every week to prevent its small trunk from bending toward the light. It also likes to be in a humid environment. Water it only when the top half of the soil is dry to the touch. Regular house temperatures are fine.

The Jerusalem cherry (*Solanum pseudocapsicum*) and the ornamental pepper (*Capsicum frutescens*) are adorable, sprightly, and fun. They come on the market in the fall but hang around as suitable holiday gifts. Bear in mind, however, that half of their life cycle is over by the time Christmas rolls around. Jerusalem cherry is happier with cooler night temperatures, down to fifty degrees is OK. The ornamental pepper likes it warmer, sixty to sixty-five degrees, in the same range with your other houseplants. Both like direct winter sunlight, four hours in a south facing window, and both should be watered when the top layer of soil feels dry. When they stop producing their showy fruits, throw them out unless you want to propagate them as an exercise in horticulture.

Speaking of horticulture, orchids are a topic unto themselves. Each species has its own needs and, if those needs are provided, the orchids will do beautifully and be among your most beloved and rewarding plants. Since we think of our plants as people, think of orchids as a family of finicky individuals who must be catered to, each in his/her own way. But when we do so, no persons are better guests!

It's All About Control

The Botany of Desire by Michael Pollan, New York, NY, Random House, 2001 is subtitled, *A Plant's-Eye View of the World*. Pollan chooses four plants to illustrate the interrelationship of botanical and human life. The book makes the case that those four plants, among many others, influenced the course of history, which they did and still do, but the reverse is also true. The ways in which humans used and still use those plants not only reveal our wisdom and weaknesses but also influence the continued survival and well being of the plants themselves.

Each of the four plants is linked to a basic human desire, the apple with sweetness, the tulip with beauty, marijuana with intoxication, and the potato with control. Beginning with John Chapman, a.k.a. Johnny Appleseed, and ending with Monsanto Corporation, we learn how man, while he is planting, pollinating, hybridizing, controlling, in other words acting like a "human bumblebee," as the author puts it, is really controlled by the plants themselves while he unwittingly aids them in their long journey of evolution.

The author has grown each of these plants in his own garden and can speak from firsthand experience and observation. Not all of us can do that. Most of us lack the space for an apple orchard or a potato field, lack the skill to hybridize tulips to the breaking point, and certainly lack the courage to buck the law and try a few *Cannabis Sativa X Indica*!

But we don't need to have raised these plants to appreciate the author's humorous biographies. We can picture the Johnny Appleseed he describes, a sort of Ohio River bum, spreading his apple seeds not for fruit but for the applejack so intensely desired on the frontier. We can relate to the Dutch and other Europeans of the late 1500s who spent fortunes on the latest tulip, unaware that they were enabling a virus, even as we spend fortunes on the fad of the moment. Every college kid who has tried to grow a few marijuana plants will sympathize with the author's anguish as his plants behind the garage are almost discovered by the local chief of police ... a close call that resulted in his destroying his own crop. And the controversy over genetically modified crops takes on additional meaning with Pollan's account of his visit to Idaho potato growers.

I have been thinking about the book's premise, that plants and humans help each other to survive, and how it can be applied even to plants in pots.

A plant in a pot is a prisoner. It's all about control. That philodendron or begonia is totally dependent on me for its care and, ultimately, its survival. Its roots are encased in a medium from which it cannot escape, its rate of growth is influenced (in cooperation with its genetic instructions) by the amount of food and water I give it, and its general state of health is determined by the environment of its living quarters.

But who is really in control? The plant will perform well, and reward the keeper, only if it is content. Someone had to do a good potting job just to get it started. As the roots outgrow the space originally allotted, the prisoner needs a larger cell. If this is denied, the plant will register its discontent in some way which, most probably, will not be attractive.

If I neglect to feed and water it, the plant will send me strong signals. Drooping stems, yellowing or browning, withering leaves, and refusal to flower are all methods this control freak will employ. And if its quarters are too dark or too bright, too cold or too hot, or too windy or too stagnant, it will react with some statement of complaint that will get it the attention it needs if it is to continue to perform its role as a happy houseplant.

Thinking of our plants as people is part of our human responsibility here, but beyond that is the suggestion that even plants in pots are continuing to act upon us as their ancestors have. For example, if a certain cultivar does not perform well as a houseplant, what happens? Breeders

get to work to determine what genes will produce a better philodendron or begonia, one
that will require less light or that will endure
more stress or that will produce more flowers.
Lo and behold, we have a better buy on the
market. Who will buy an ivy that is a problem
when you can buy an ivy that isn't? In this
way, the ivy has secured a place for itself in the
chain of evolution that assures its survival, at
least for the moment, until a better ivy comes
along.

This interdependence is very obvious in
today's flower horticulture. Bigger has been
better, doubles have been more popular than singles, the more variety of
color the more popular the species. But now there is a movement back
to the originals, the little single roses, flowers that have scent, and native
plants that perform well under adverse conditions because they are used to
them. Here again, various species are ensuring their survival by endearing
themselves to us, the planters and caregivers.

So Pollan's "plant's-eye view of the world" can be seen from the pot
as well as from the cultivated garden, fruit orchard, or open field. Every houseplant has its origins in nature, somewhere on the planet. There,
whether in the tropical rainforests of South America or on windswept
mountainsides in Asia, these plants learned the art of survival and subse-
quently got themselves collected and brought to the "civilized" countries
of Europe and America. As we nourish them and presume to improve
them, they use us as aids in their own process of evolution.

Not much has changed.

About the Author

Philodendron
squamiferum

Anne Moore is a freelance writer and amateur horticulturist. Her interest in houseplants and container gardening has provided subjects for her column, In the Pot, appearing in newspapers and online, and for numerous magazine articles. Moore is a graduate of Wellesley College where she did not major in botany, but she has educated herself about plants through courses offered by the many horticultural organizations in New England, and by trial and error in her own indoor and outdoor gardens. She is a member of the Garden Club of Brookline, a former trustee of the New England Wild Flower Society, and a member of the Steering Committee of the Wellesley College Friends of Horticulture. She has been an annual exhibitor and award winner in the New England Spring Flower Show sponsored by the Massachusetts Horticultural Society. She has homes in both New Hampshire and Arizona, where she lives with her husband and plants.

"Learning about my plants, and caring for them, has given me enormous pleasure and endless subjects to write about."

Website: www.annemooreplants.com

About the Artist

Gloxinia

Rebecca Saunders is an artist and photographer who captures the colors and textures of the natural world, whether in a greenhouse or garden, at home or traveling. She has done the line drawings for this book directly from plants in her own collection and from photographs she has taken.

"A camera gives me quick satisfaction; a sketch or painting puts it more permanently in my mind."

CPSIA information can be obtained at www.ICGtesting.com
Printed in the USA
BVOW021626121012

302703BV00007B/13/P